Chapter 1

Tess

The Mystery of Enlightenment

You have heard this word 'Enlightenment' before? Of course you have. Possibly only when hearing of The Buddha and even the stories of the old Eastern Masters levitating and walking through walls. Perhaps you have been reading about Enlightenment for some time and, if this is the case, the fact that you are reading this book suggests that you still have questions unanswered. Why is this? Go to any internet discussion forum on the subject and you are likely to find many individuals, quite knowledgeable on the subject, discussing and even arguing as to what it is, and often whether or not it even exists at all. Some accept only The Buddha himself as ever being Enlightened (The story of The Buddha, meaning 'Enlightened One', tells of a young prince who left his palace to see so much misery outside that he longed to find the truth of it. He travelled for many years trying out various methods and teachings. None satisfied him until one day he sat down under a tree alone and in the silence within found what has been called 'Nirvana'). Some say one cannot truly be Enlightened whilst alive and others, having spent their whole adult life searching and seeming to have made very little progress, say it does not really exist at all.

So what is it? What is this thing they call Enlightenment that is causing so much debate and confusion? And why does it cause so much debate and confusion? The answer to the latter is because it is beyond the experience of the thinking mind and emotions. That is to say, no matter how hard you think about it, no matter how intelligent you are and how many books you read or people you talk to, you cannot truly know what Enlightenment is. And even if you do become Enlightened, again, because it is beyond the understandings of even your own mind and emotions, it is then subject to your own interpretations when you look at it and put it into words for others to understand.

So where does that leave us? We are left with what Enlightenment is? I can only answer this in my own experience and again I ask you to listen/read and feel inside, and deny the imagination from trying to interpret the words. Whatever you turn the words into will not be the truth. Just read the words and feel whatever you do. Enlightenment is your own space inside that you are feeling. If there is disturbance or indeed any other sensation there, that is not it. Enlightenment is the space supporting and surrounding it. That may not mean much to you right now, which is the reason why so few are Enlightened and why it is so hard to explain or understand. The thinking mind looks to work things out, to dissect things and put them back together to see how they function. The emotions look to feel themselves, be it happiness or anger or jealousy or any other wanting or trying. The space you are feeling inside you, where there is no feeling, has nothing for the mind to think about or for the emotions to feel. So, for anyone looking for the answers and wanting to be Enlightened, it could be a pretty big let down if they were permitted to find it before they were ready, and therefore they continue to spend the rest of their lives looking for 'something'. But again, looking for what? That's the whole point! ...isn't it? They are looking for this mystical state of being which is meant to be the end of all striving and worry and the end of all questions, but the one place it is, there is nothing there!

This is why Enlightenment is so simple (I say) and yet so rare. I will describe in more detail about this state of being, what it is, and how to become it.

What is Enlightenment?

Some believe it is becoming 'One' with the universe. Some say it is achieving 'God Consciousness' or 'Christ Consciousness' or 'God Realisation' or 'Self Realisation' or 'Self Actualisation'. Some say it is living in the moment. Some say it is living in the now. Some say it is seeing through the illusion, that there is nobody really here and that nothing is real. Others simply say it is living without problems or worries, perhaps due to all the above. The list could probably go on with the many different views, ideas and stories as to what it really is.

So, which ones are true? And perhaps more so, how do we know which ones are true, or even if the person telling us which ones are true is really Enlightened? Especially if we have just established it is hard enough even for the Enlightened person to describe what it is in words that others can understand; so what chance do we stand of telling whether or not they are speaking the truth?

I am going to take you into the experience throughout this book and by the end you should be in very little doubt as to what it truly is. You will then be able to speak from your own experience, but not because you will be Enlightened necessarily since, while you will be able to see the truth of it and glimpse the reality, remaining in it for any length of time is not always easy. However, you will also know it does not actually matter whether you are Enlightened or not. Your only responsibility, to you and to life, is to be you, as honest and aware as you can be at any moment. There is nothing else you need to try to be, and nowhere else you need to try to go, other than where you are now. Of course in the next moment you may indeed be somewhere else, but at any moment you can only be where you are.

Different Teachings

For those that accept it as real, there are many teachers and teachings that claim to offer the answers as to how to reach it. Many involve some sort of meditation, which is often concentration on the breath, or on a repeated word or phrase or an imagined image; all with the aim of calming the mind to silence the endless chatter and imaginings that go on, and on, and on. Others we know of involve strenuous physical exercise, such as some of the Buddhist Monks we see performing marvellous feats of endurance. Some teachers even teach that there is nothing at all you can do, with the explanation that either it will happen or it won't as all is 'God's will', or that you are already Enlightened so there is nothing you need to do, and/or even that there is nobody here anyway to even be, or not to be Enlightened.

Again there are perhaps many other teachings and techniques available, but I am not going to confuse you by describing all those, only to tell you later to forget them. I am going to take you into the simplest most direct way, certainly that I have come across. It is the way I did it and where I am as I describe it. That is to say, I could have attempted to describe what I was doing while I was doing it, but the experience and knowledge would have been limited to where I was at that time. Now I talk from the experience of having used a definite method and technique to get to where I am now, and talk from here. That does not only mean I have been through it, it means I am all the way through it. I know the hold ups and the tricks the mind can throw up to confuse you and to talk you out of what you are doing here. And what are you doing here? So far I have only asked you to remain aware of where you are and of what you are feeling inside, in the space where there is little or no feeling and all is well. Keep doing this as we go further.

The Simple Way

So, on with business. I told you I was going to show you the most simple and direct path to Enlightenment. I also told you it was possible your mind would want to analyse, question and even spoil what I am going to show you. I ask that you do your very best to just stay open and stay aware.

The basic theory behind the method is this: If you accept the idea that there is one intelligence here, some sort of greater consciousness or God behind everything, some omnipotent being, then where is the best place to look for such an intelligence? Keeping in mind intelligence itself cannot be seen so only the effects of it can, and if we accept there is an intelligence behind everything, then this is all the effect of this intelligence, is it not? Therefore, there is little point in measuring or digging up or going out into space or splitting the atom to find this intelligence, as everything is just the effect of the same intelligence and we would just be looking at more effects. So again, where we do we look? This is the blatantly obvious part (it is if you don't allow the mind to spoil it). If there is truly one intelligence behind everything, and you are intelligent (at least enough to know you are here) where is this intelligence? YOU ARE IT!! Is that simple enough?

And having accepted the idea that there is perhaps one intelligence behind everything, and you are it, what now? Now you just feel it. In fact that is what I have been asking you to do since you opened this book. Just be aware of where you are and of what you are feeling. This is you, before you imagine you are something, label anything and begin thinking about who you are, what you've done and what you should be doing etc. This is the simple way.

How to practise

In essence, you just keep doing what I have said. Keep as aware as you can each and every moment.

Are you beginning to wonder if this is some sort of con? You have paid for this book having been told it will be the answer to all the mystery, and all it tells you to do is to be aware of where you are. Was it all just fancy talk to get you to buy the book?

I can assure you this is no con, but it is so simple your mind will try to talk you out of it. 'That won't work', it will tell you, '...so don't even try'. It will do its damndest to convince you the only way is struggle and effort and endless searching and analysing and questioning. Because what I am showing you is the way, the way to become what you are behind the endless chatter and the emotions going up and down with each experience, the mind does not want you to do it. And if you do listen to it, you won't do it. But what won't you do? I have only asked you to be aware of where you are and of what you are feeling. What is so scary about that? Why on earth are your emotions squirming? (if indeed they are). Can you see this surely cannot do any harm, even if it doesn't work to Enlighten you, what can it hurt to practice being aware of where you are and of what you are feeling? Of course the truth is it can't. However, you have never done it for very long, which is why you are not Enlightened (let's say), and the only thing preventing you from being Enlightened is that little voice or feeling telling you to think about something else and imagine being somewhere else; in fact trying to put your attention anywhere but here, where you are!!! Can you see this? Can you see how you are looking for the truth behind what you are and yet have spent all your life imagining and thinking about being somewhere else doing something else?

The reason it is so difficult is due to the need for experience, the need to feel. That is the need that has created this whole existence anyway and without it none of this would be here. So don't worry about it too much (and it wouldn't help you anyway). The space you feel is clearly you inside, but why is there no feeling there? The reason is simply, because it is YOU. Can you see this? When you go to feel what you already are, you cannot feel it because you are already there. The space is you.

This is likely to be new to you because here we deal with sensation through which to experience anything. And yet the sensation is only possible because you are feeling something separate from you. By feeling inside where you are aware only of a stillness, or even just the knowledge 'I am' if the stillness is too fine to feel, you are in touch with your true being. Keep doing this and you are on the path to Enlightenment. The truth is you always were, because one way or another all ends up back here. It is just good if you can do it while you are alive, now.

The rest of the book will take you further into this, address many of the difficulties that can be thrown up and describe how to deal with these. For the ease of writing and saving me from having to qualify each statement, I am going to take it that you do not think you are Enlightened.

What is stopping you?

I am imagining by now you have spent a little time trying to remain aware of where you are and of what you are feeling, and are not finding it easy (though it may be easier to do this while you are reading this book). What is it that prevents you from staying aware of yourself, and what can you do about it?

Again this is simple, as is the solution. We have said it is the need for experience which keeps things moving here; in fact it keeps everything here. Your mind feels the space inside and perhaps for a split second you may feel a relaxation or a sense of the peace; but that is only for a split second before the mind steps in with 'Yes, but..' or something else, just to interrupt you and take you away. You will then be in your imagination, thinking about where you have been or what you have been doing, of what has happened or might happen, or what you want or don't want. It doesn't matter what it is. The fact is, it has taken you away from being you and you are lost in your imagination. The mind is a little like an oil tanker, in the sense that it can take quite a while to really slow down, but you must start now. Otherwise it will just keep going. Each time you bring yourself back to being aware of where you are and of what you are feeling, it will be that little easier next time. The space has its own power. The more you feel it and the more you want to feel it, the more you will find it seems to wake you up. You will be merrily thinking about something and suddenly you will be aware you are thinking. Then you have a choice. You can carry on thinking, or stop, drop the thought (as it's not real anyway) and come back to your senses. Each time you do this (let go of the thought to return to your senses) puts a little more space between you and the thinking and a little closer to being what you truly are, and always have been, behind the thinking, feeling and imaginings. How long does this take? ...Well, you are doing it now, aren't you? How long did that take? Admittedly the whole process is a lifetime process. Even once you are Enlightened enough to know and live the truth, the process still continues as you are still here. It is then the same process, except by that stage you are not trying to become Enlightened any more to realise the Truth as you are living the truth, or even you are The Living Truth. But the process of living out the need to be here continues to the end.

Feelings

You may be asking, 'What is the point of feeling the space inside when there is nothing there to feel?' And of course you'd be right. This is what I meant when I mentioned earlier that you may begin to see it is not better to be Enlightened. There is nothing here. The path to Enlightenment may take you down a road of many experiences and insights and flashes of white light (if it does). You may have sensations of expanding or contracting, of being extremely tall, or tiny. You may be given psychic experiences or visions of other realms or higher realities. You may indeed be given any number of these or other experiences not mentioned here, but in the end what have you got? You are still you. You still have your problems and your worries and your regrets, you still hate this or like that and have all your questions as to what it is all about and who are you? Feelings only lead to more feelings. Questions lead to more questions. If you want to find the point where there are no more questions, where everything is complete and at peace, well you now know where it is! You don't have to spend any more time there than you do, but it is there, within you, and it is your true being behind all your efforts and trying; always waiting for you to return when you are ready.

That is the point here. There is nothing you have to do until you are ready. The reason existence is here is due to the need for experience, so I am not surprised at people who don't want, or aren't ready, to feel the space inside where there is little or no experience. Why should you? After all, as I said, that is why you are here. Having said that, I must bring you back to the fact the feelings do not last. They come and go, hurt and confuse you, blame and accuse you and others, all just to get some more feeling. I ask you, if you are of the above view (that feelings are good), to look at this the next time you are feeling bad and at the fact that you are defending your right to your feelings. When you feel bad and are blaming someone else or something else for making you feel bad, whilst wallowing in your self-made justification for feeling that way, just have a look at who is really responsible for how you are feeling. Is it the person or situation that is to blame for how you feel? Or is it you who has chosen to feel that way? The fact that you are too irresponsible to do anything about it does not take away the fact that you are responsible. This is indeed your life and you are the one living it. If you are interested in Enlightenment, even mildly, it may be of use to you to at least look at the idea that sometimes you may feel bad because you want to, not because you have to.

Dealing with Problems

Everybody seems to have problems. That is, things in their life that upset and disturb them. Things they seem to have hanging around and just won't seem to go away, and often as soon as one does go away another is in its place. How does this idea of 'being aware of where you are and of what you are feeling' help in any way in dealing with these problems? Wouldn't it make it harder if you stopped thinking about them and imagining them? Isn't that avoiding them and not dealing with them?

The short answer is, the opposite is the case. The reason people have so many problems, the reason you have so many problems, if you do, is exactly because you spend your time thinking and worrying about them instead of either accepting things as they are, for now at least, or taking the action you are avoiding. By that I mean, you have a problem which is either something you cannot change, for now, in which case you need to accept it for now; or you know there is some action you should take and are putting it off for some reason, perhaps through fear, and therefore it won't go away. And of course it won't go away while you know there is something you need to do and you aren't doing it!! The disturbance inside you is telling you something is not right. Why do you go through your life accepting it? Why do you lie awake at night imagining what you could do and wishing things were different, or going through each day burdened with all these problems, and just accepting this?

Of course the reason you accept it is because everybody else does, and that is what you have been taught; after all, everybody has problems, don't they? Well, guess what, I don't! Yes, you heard correctly. I don't have any problems! The next question is perhaps, why don't I? Why or how am I so special that I don't have any problems? And of course if this is true, how can you get rid of yours?

Again, this is very simple. Once again your mind and emotions are likely to talk you out of it, and say 'Oh yeah, that's interesting, but wouldn't work for me', or something similar. But will you try it? Or will you accept your mind when it tells you not to bother? All I ask you to do is be aware of where you are and of what you are feeling. This is what happens at present....

Something happens in your life and you feel a strong emotional disturbance inside you. This causes you to imagine the situation and think about it, and think about it, and think about it, and think about it. After a while you feel exhausted and the thinking stops, until later it returns again, and again. I think we both have to agree that is not very constructive?!

What I suggest you do, is this... when you first feel the disturbance, feel your breathing and your body and see where you are physically. This prevents you from getting lost in the emotional imaginary world where nothing gets done. While holding knowledge of the problem and feeling the emotion and still staying aware of your body and where you are, have a look at what you can see are your options to address the problem. You were peaceful and all was ok until this arose, and you want to be in that peace again. Therefore you will do whatever you have to do in order to satisfy the mind that you have done all you can (yes?).

As you look at your options, you may see there are a number of things you could do and, if so, you can only pick the one that feels the most 'right'. There may be only one which you know you must do, or there may be options but none of them are 'right' at this time. Once you have either taken the action, or feel at this time there is nothing you can or should do, just hold onto your awareness (aware that you exist) and feel the emotion squirm. Feel as it pushes and struggles to make you go into the imagination and relive and imagine the problem. It does not want you to do anything to fix it, Oh no! The emotion just wants you to wallow in the problem in your imagination. You do not want that any more! You will find it is very clever. As you are holding the knowledge of what is wrong and denying yourself from actually thinking about it, you may find you are soon thinking about something else unrelated, just so the emotion can get its foot in the door and soon, before you know it, you are thinking about the problem you are trying not to think about. That's ok. Just bring yourself back to feeling your breathing (which serves to calm the mind initially) and back to the awareness of your senses, aware of where you are and of what you are feeling.

That's it. You will feel after a little while, the emotion beginning to have less force and the problem seems less in some way; and later that day you will notice it has gone totally, but you are not sure when. It may have taken some time to get to this stage, all the time you were feeling really uncomfortable inside and knowing why, but still not allowing yourself to actually think about and get lost in the imagination of the problem.

Once the feeling has gone, have a look at the situation that was disturbing you and you will see either it has changed and is no longer a problem, or it has not actually changed, but it was never a problem anyway. What has happened here is your emotional attachment to the situation could not survive in you when you would not think about the situation, so perished; and this is the story of all emotional disturbance and pain. Emotion cannot survive without the imagination to feed it. Initially it rises on its own when an uncomfortable thought occurs to you or something happens outside to wake it up, because it was already within you waiting for an opportunity to show its ugly head. But once it's there you have a choice, either go into it and allow it to feed off you as you rant and rave or wallow in self pity or worry, or you can look practically at what can be done, take any action you see needs to be taken, and then deny the remaining emotion from taking you into its imaginary world. Each time you do this, the less pull the emotion has over you and the more conscious you are becoming. It is only the emotion within you now which has not yet been faced which is preventing you from being Enlightened at this moment. There is nothing else here. There is only the intelligence or space you are feeling within and there is the attachment or need for experience, which at 'problem times' is at its most obvious. It strives to feel more and relive and relive and relive the problem in its own little imaginary world, over and over again. It is when dealing with 'problems' that you are making the most ground towards Enlightenment, as long as you take the necessary action and do not allow the mind to go round and round.

An important point to note is, you will never be able to feel the space and dissolve and be free of the emotion connected to a problem if you do not take the action required. You will not be able to rest as you will know somewhere inside you that you are avoiding it. This is the simplest and most direct teaching and method I know of, but it does mean you have to do something. That something is only to be honest with your self. If something is disturbing you, DO NOT ACCEPT THE DISTURBANCE. You must accept the situation and let it go if you can, but if you cannot let it go then you must take some action; and if there is nothing you can do at this time then you have no choice but to accept the situation as it is, for now. You will come to see, but perhaps take on faith for now, that as there is only one intelligence here and you are that, your own emotional state of mind directly effects what happens in your life. This is true responsibility. The circumstances of your life are here to teach you and to give you whatever it is you need, not necessarily what you think you want. So far in your life you have wanted experience, and of course that is what you have had. You know now it hurts. ...Not always, but it does! You have allowed your emotions to drag you away each time as you didn't know there was another way, and as such they have become so strong that you are barely in control or aware of where you are at any time. Often you may not even be aware that you being emotional. Now you are going to change. You are the boss here now, not the feelings. It just takes some vigilance before the metaphorical employee is back in line.

What is happening is you are withdrawing from the striving for experience and beginning to spend more time in the space you are beyond and before experience, but it takes time. You have been so driven for so long it cannot happen all at once, but it can start now. The more you hold onto the awareness of where you are and what you are feeling, the more you get used to the space and the less time you spend in the imaginary world feeding the emotions.

I started off by saying I don't have any problems. Oh, I used to, many of them, until I began to do this. Almost overnight I found I only had to deal with one at a time, and that one was whatever was happening in front of me at that moment. I knew each time that it had happened to disturb me, to bring up the emotions so I could deny the imagination and dissolve them, thus making me more conscious. As I faced the emotion each time, the problem became a situation which I could deal with practically, or not as was required. The quicker I was able to let go of the emotion, the quicker a problem would become a situation which would either fix itself, or I found it was not an issue for me anyway. These days it is a little different. Life will show me a situation could occur some time before it does. I will feel a slight disturbance in me which is the little emotion that was attached to the idea of the situation going the way I wanted, and I face the emotion as described above by taking any action I see needs to be taken and not allowing the mind to think about it. Very quickly the emotion connected to the situation has gone and invariably the situation I was shown never actually happens. It was only showing me what could happen to allow me to be free of that 'piece' of emotion. Now I have done that, there is no reason for the situation to even occur at all. This may or may not happen to you in exactly this way, but the point is there. This is your life, and your problems are there to make you emotional. The more you are emotional, the more problems you get to make you more emotional. As you begin to deny the emotion the energy it needs in the imaginary world, by being aware of where you are and thinking less, the fewer problems you find you have until, you too will say, 'I don't have any problems!'.

I will add here, don't get confused between 'not having problems' and 'life no longer providing difficult situations'. The situations can still occur. The change is that the Enlightened person is able, through the above process, to face and deal with them quickly and practically, thus actually decreasing the emotion within them rather than increasing it.

"With each difficult situation comes greater consciousness".

Nick Roach

"Be aware of where you are
And of what you are feeling"

Chapter 2

Love and Consciousness

In my direction to you to 'remain as conscious and aware as you can each and every moment, of where you are and of what you are feeling', I have given you the only real tool you need to reach Enlightenment, if that is still what you want. However, I am aware also of the mind's need to have answers to its questions, or at least to know there are answers. That is until it reaches the end of the answers, (but we will look at that later). One question it is likely to ask is relating to love and how love fits into this 'feeling the space with no feeling' stuff?

Again, it's very simple. Stay with me as usual, and be aware of the chair and the room etc, and of any feeling, or lack of, within you.

When you love someone, there is a feeling of being complete when you are with them and, when you are not with them, you can 'miss' them, or feel you have a piece of yourself missing. Can you see where this is going already? We have said there is one intelligence here, and the space you feel inside is it. However, you feel you are separate from this most of the time. When you 'love' somebody, their form is acting as a mirror for you to reflect off allowing you to feel a part of yourself you don't usually, thus you feel complete. When they go away, you no longer have the reflection and therefore feel you have a piece missing. That's the essence of love, your own being reflected back to you by an external form.

The way to use it properly, to grow in consciousness and love, is again to remain aware. Aware of where you are, aware of any feeling in you, and aware of your knowledge of the person you love. You will see it is exactly the same process as when dealing with problems in the sense that, by remaining aware, you are denying the imagination from carrying you away. Even though you are not with the person at this moment (let's say) you are feeling inside where you love them and where you are complete, so you don't feel incomplete. Thus you can love someone all the time, even when not with them, and still not miss them; not because you don't love them, but because you do! You just choose to hold onto the knowledge inside where you love them and where you are complete, rather than let go of the love and go into your imagination where there is only emotion and pain, and thus you would feel incomplete.

You may be beginning to see how simple, and yet how effective and even logical this all is. At present you are likely to spend much of your life in your imagination, thinking and worrying about things that may or may not happen, or have already happened, and then wonder what it is all about and who you are. The simple truth is, you are where and what you have always been, right where you feel 'I am' inside you; where there is no feeling because you are already there and you feel complete and whole because you are complete and whole (that is until you leave it to imagine being somewhere else doing something else, only to wonder why you now feel so separate and incomplete).

Sex versus Making Love

Having touched on love in the last chapter, and on feelings and the lack of them before that, I anticipated you may have a question in you regarding Sex. That is, 'How do you have sex with no emotional feelings and no imagination?' The answer is, 'You don't!'

'Shock!'... 'Am I telling you to be celibate now?' No, absolutely not! I am just introducing you to the difference between Sex and Making Love, which you very possibly have never heard before except perhaps in fairytale fantasies which you have long since convinced yourself are only that, so stay with me.

We all know about Sex. One needs to be 'in the mood' for it, needs to get turned on and excited, often with some sort of games and teasing to raise the anticipation. If it goes well, then both parties become excited and together their feelings take them away into a whirlwind of excitement, until the orgasm when all ends. At this point both are satisfied, and one or both get up and go to do something, or just roll over in little or no acknowledgement of the other and go to sleep. If it is not so mutually enjoyable, as in many cases, the woman may just lie back while the man enjoys himself with her pretending, or not, to be enjoying it; until he has relieved himself inside her. At which time he does roll over and go to sleep, leaving her wide awake feeling used and unloved. If she is able to, she may be able to imagine the man having sex with her is another, possibly totally mythical man, who is truly loving her, thus giving her some feeling of enjoyment, albeit imagined. In some situations the man may have been with this woman for so long the excitement went ages ago for him too, so now it is more of a physical release and his feelings can also be helped along by imagining being with someone else. So, this is Sex huh?! This is what you are asking me about? Now let me talk to you about Making Love.

We have looked at what love is. Love is the stillness and completeness inside that you feel, and you are most aware of it when it is newly reflected by another. That is to say, it is a part of yourself you don't usually feel, so you feel more complete when you are with this person. Eventually, when you are aware all the time, you could be said to be in a state of love all the time; but not because you love in an emotional sense, but because you are always feeling complete and whole and everything becomes your reflection. So, if that is love, what do you think Making Love could be? Making Love must be the process of making you more conscious, more complete and more in touch with the space inside you; and that is exactly what happens if done properly.

Instead of all the usual practices of sex, in Making Love the two people come together physically, but both totally aware of where they are and of what they are feeling. By doing this, it prevents the mind from running off ahead and imagining what they are about to do, and therefore keeping the feelings of excitement out. This is good for the man who usually has trouble controlling himself, because the less emotional excitement he has, the less his orgasm is likely to come too early. It also means he is able to appreciate the woman more even if they have been together for some time, as he is not so absorbed in himself or the feelings of routine. He had been looking past her for so long, having lost the spark of attraction in their life of familiarity. Now he is conscious and sees his woman new. He has no need to get excited. In fact excitement is selfish anyway. Your excitement is no good for you to love the other person, and their excitement does not love you. Sex and excitement is just about taking, to satisfy the emotional need for personal gratification, until it comes up again for more.

This Making Love is very different. Because the man is more aware of himself and of the woman, she knows he is there for her and to love and enjoy and really appreciate her. Therefore she is more likely to remain conscious and not try to go off in her own imaginary world of excitement. So now we have both parties totally aware of where they are and what they are feeling, as they hold, caress and Make Love, slowly and with no impatience or grabbing for oneself; just conscious love. The man will find, as soon as he allows himself to think about and imagine where he is rather than just feeling, he is likely to lose control and orgasm early, so he must remain aware and stop or even withdraw if he feels it is too strong and he is not ready, or they are not ready.

As you practice this with your partner, and it does take both parties to do this (If one is trying to love while the other is looking to just take for himself or herself, or is just there through a feeling of obligation or routine, it clearly will not work.) you will find a whole new world. You will no longer need to 'be in the mood' to make love, as you are always open to love. You will also find it lasts longer and is invariably (will become 'always') mutually fulfilling. The sensation is one of intense peace, stillness and pleasure as you consciously love and are loved. There is a mutual sharing of conscious energies which remain long after making love has finished. Whatever experience happens it is all shared, and the sensations grow in both parties simultaneously, every time. Once you and your partner are able to enjoy and love in total conscious awareness, the feelings grow in both easily and they feel as one. In fact, it can feel you are merging into each other, losing the boundaries where one ends and the other begins, yet both remain totally conscious.

On a more serious note, (not that the rest wasn't serious, but just more positive) the last part has some reality even with sex. Just as the energies grow together in making conscious love, the energies still transfer in sex. Women know this as the connection they often feel having slept with a man, as if a part of him is left behind; and it is. If he is selfish, aggressive or emotional and taking for himself in any way, he will leave behind some of his emotion and lack of love within the body/psyche of the woman, thus making her more unhappy and feeling less love/conscious and with more separation inside her. The yearning in her grows more and more for the connection as each sexual encounter takes her further from the conscious love she seeks. A woman may think a man feels the same way as she does and it has been known for her to try to get a man into bed to catch him, only to find it worked in getting him into bed but he was gone by morning; or equally bad, he just comes back for sex whenever he wants it. You cannot get a man to love you by offering him sexual gratification. Love is consciousness and appreciation. Make sure he loves you before you let him inside you, because if he doesn't love you when he's outside, how the hell do you expect him to love and appreciate you once he's getting what he wants inside?

So, once again we come back to remaining aware of where you are and of what you are feeling. This is the way to Enlightenment and the way to realise and become your true being behind the mind and emotions. It takes you into the peace behind your feelings and enables you to deal with problems, even to the point of no longer having any. It enables you to love and Make Love so you are complete and at peace all the time, and every time you Make Love is perfect as you and your partner are growing in conscious love together, becoming the reality behind the myth of Adam and Eve in the Garden of Eden. (Do you think the last part was a little over the top? It's happened for me and my partner. It can happen to you).

In case you have ever wondered what the word 'Tantra' means, it is this (as described above). But just as Making Love has been degraded into Sex, the true meaning of Tantra has been lost and denigrated into the 'Hollywood' idea of extended sex sessions with greater and greater sexual gratification and selfish excitement.

Making Plans

I have been asked before, 'How do you make plans if you stay aware now and do not go into your imagination? Surely you must, or you would never get anything done!'

Do not get 'looking at something intelligently' mixed up with the thinking process that goes over and over and round and round, regurgitating the same thoughts and feelings for entertainment sake and getting nothing done.

Let's say you need to make plans to go on holiday. You go to the travel agent or look on the internet, or whatever you do, and while you do so you are aware of where you are and of what you are doing. You choose which appeals the most and ensure you can pay for it and a car etc is arranged, and if not you arrange it. You look calmly and practically at all the arrangements to ensure nothing is missed or overlooked, wherever possible. Once booked, you then no longer think about it and instead get on with something else. The usual way is to go into the imagination and feelings and now, having lost touch with the stillness and peace, find you get excited or worried or something else. You then relive the imaginings for the next few weeks or months until the time for the holiday comes, very rarely being aware of where you are so your mind is often not on the job at hand.

Once we get on holiday, the usual way is to always look forward to the next thing we are going to do, or think about what we have already done. We look forward to going to the beach, or for a swim, or going to the club, or even going to sleep; always looking for the next experience, or remembering and reliving the last.

I am asking you to just be aware of where you are and of what you are feeling. Not only does it mean your full attention is on the job at hand so you are more likely to do an efficient job, but also you find you are able to appreciate and enjoy each moment, before, during and after, without looking forward or back.

When making the plans, you are aware of what you are doing. When waiting to go on the holiday, instead of thinking about it you remain aware of where you are and of what you are doing, thus able to enjoy the time as it passes. Then you get to your holiday and enjoy the whole experience of getting to the airport, getting on the plane, arriving, unpacking, going to the beach, swimming, going out, staying in, packing again and even coming home and returning to work. All becomes a conscious flowing experience of enjoyment where you put your full attention into whatever you are doing and the things you do are more likely to be correct. You do not look for the feeling of the next or the last experience to fulfil you, as inside where you feel the space you are always complete. You do not go on holiday to 'get away' in the usual sense as you enjoy your life whether you are on holiday or at work, or whatever you are doing. Just be aware of where you are and of what you are feeling. This helps you to be more efficient and enjoy what you are doing more, whatever it is, in the moment.

Standing up for Yourself

I have also been asked, and the question may have occurred to you, 'If I stay in a feeling of peace all the time, won't people just walk all over me? Surely I have to get annoyed at times in order to stand up for myself?'

Good question, if you are not being honest! …I will explain. Normally you may be inclined to put up with something until you are so annoyed that you explode, or you may just explode at the first instance because it has happened to you so many times before that you are not prepared for it to happen again. Neither response is particularly fair on the person you are attacking, because either you were too irresponsible to speak up the first time they did whatever it was that upset you, or you had too little self-control not to over-react the first time. So by remaining aware as much as you can, whatever you are doing, of where you are and of what you are feeling, you are able to spot any disturbance early instead of ignoring it or exploding in anger. Then you can treat it like any other problem and look quickly at what can be done. Perhaps a quiet light hearted few words to the person to let them know what they did makes you uncomfortable will be enough for them to be more aware, to apologise, and not do it again. Perhaps they will explain why they did it and you may see they were actually correct. Or they may ignore you totally, in which case next time you are able to speak more firmly as you have already asked and informed them once. You may even see it as appropriate to explode the first time, but at least you do so consciously and not through lack of control.

The point is again to be aware; to feel the space inside where you are aware that you exist, as much as you can, and protect this space with whatever tools you have. You can then address any disturbance as soon as it arises to see where it came from, why it is here now and what can you do about it? This is your life. Do not make anyone else responsible for your life by blaming them for how you feel. Either accept it or change it, but your feelings are yours; both to hold on to and yours to face and get rid of. This is your life and not the life of the person who just looked at you in a funny way, made a comment, or always says something to you that annoys you. This is your life. You live it!

As you practice this you become increasingly aware of the peace inside and your life becomes easier. At the slightest disturbance you are there and looking to address the problem practically and quickly. You do not just accept and ignore it and, once dealt with, the rest of the time you are likely to have no problems and no worries. All you need to do is just practice being aware of where you are and of what you are feeling and do not accept any disturbance unless you have looked very carefully at what you can do. If there is nothing at this time you can do, accept this for now, but keep looking to see if something changes. The simple fact that you are aware and looking to take action as soon as you are able will ensure the situation will not remain for ever. Remember there is an intelligence creating all this, and it is within you. Your own state of mind now determines what happens next.

Speeding up the Solution

Sometimes we seem to have the same problem for ages. This is because we have not learnt the lesson it is there to teach, or we are not responsible enough to make the changes required to address the problem; which in turn translates into still not having learnt the lesson life is there to teach us. All your life is about teaching you to be responsible for your own life (or allowing you to enjoy the ignorance of not being). The more you are able to be conscious and responsible for your life, the quicker you learn the lessons and the quicker each problem becomes a situation, which in turn is resolved. If however you are quite content, without admitting to that of course, to be irresponsible and hold to blaming everybody else but yourself for your life, you will be stuck with a life of troubles and torment. Sometimes hard, at other times perhaps not so hard, but all the time your life and your feelings will be at the mercy of your environment – which you will not be aware is of your own creation anyway.

Most people would say they are looking for peace of some sort. You are reading this book which is entitled 'Enlightenment, The simple path' so I imagine you are interested in the peace Enlightenment offers. The first thing to learn, after being aware of where you are and of what you are feeling all the time, is you, and you alone, are responsible for your life. The sooner you accept this, the sooner your life will become more of an obstacle-course or play-ground, perfectly designed for you to learn and grow; rather than the usual mismatch of problems and struggles which you may currently accept as unavoidable and cope with by looking forward and back to better times

Paying for Everything

There is a common phrase that says you must pay for everything, and to that many people are inclined to reply something along the lines of 'you don't pay for happiness!' Well, let's look at this for a moment.

Let's say you have something, perhaps a new car, which you are really excited about and proud of. Then it gets scratched or marked, or someone spills something or drops a cigarette burning the seat. The extent to which you were excited in a positive way is the extent to which you will be unhappy or angry in a negative way. 'What goes up must come down' is indeed true, certainly when dealing with emotions and feelings. To the extent you are happy, excited or looking forward to anything is the extent to which you must have the same force of negativity later, and although it is not always to do with the same situation, it often is. You don't have to accept this, and certainly your emotions are not likely to like hearing it, but everything, especially feelings, MUST be paid for. What goes up must come down. Just watch (as you are doing anyway now) and see if you get excited about something going your way, and watch as later something goes wrong to 'scupper' your plans and you feel down again. They call this 'Sod's Law' amongst other names and indeed it is a law. It is the law where this is your life and you get what you want. You want feelings? ...You will get them. But it just so happens that you can't choose to only have the positive ones. Once you create the positive you create the negative, one follows the other.

So revel in the excitement and looking forward to things if you are moved to, but be aware there are laws here. Although there are no punishments for breaking them, you just create opposites which create their own punishment, in this existence of conflicts.

Wanting & Trying

I thought it may be worth looking at the truth behind these two very common words and experiences. We all say we want this or that and we are trying to do this or that. Often we are referring to a feeling inside of discomfort as we struggle to achieve what we want or are trying to do.

When you want something, I suggest to you what you really want is to be free of the feeling inside of wanting the thing. Once you have what you want, you believe you will be satisfied and will not want anymore. Of course this is not the case and almost as soon as you get what you want, after at best a very short while of being satisfied, either the thing is not what you thought it was or you quickly want something else.

'Trying' is very similar. You feel dissatisfied with things as they are and believe that by trying to do something you will be satisfied. Again what happens is either you are more disappointed when you do not achieve what you are trying to achieve, or you do achieve it but when you get it you find it is not what you thought; or you even find it is just what you thought but you are now too busy trying to achieve the next thing to sit back and enjoy and appreciate what you have. The answer, as usual, is the same...

By remaining aware of where you are and of what you are feeling, now and always (though it takes practice), you find, at this moment now, you feel complete and at peace. There is nothing you want and there is no trying to do anything. Of course if there is, you will get up and take the action, aware and conscious of what you are doing and then sit back down still aware and conscious. This way, doing or not doing becomes a conscious thing in the moment now. You find you can indeed try to achieve something, or want something, but there is no emotional attachment to attaining the goal. You just do what you can. That does not have to translate into being lazy or disinterested, because you are putting your full attention into the process, unlike even those who are trying to achieve or want who may still be split as they are trying to achieve and want many things. At any moment you are only doing one thing, 100% ...like now.

So, you begin to see by being here now, aware of where you are and of what you are feeling, you want and try less but can achieve more. However, the main achievement is actually in the being aware of where you are and of what you are feeling. There is nothing greater you can achieve. All else that occurs is just living the dream, whilst the feeling of the space inside you is ‘waking up’.

"Be aware of where you are
And of what you are feeling"

Chapter 3

Going Deeper

We have looked at what you can do to become Enlightened and some of the other areas in your life that are helped, not hindered, by the practice of simply being aware of where you are and of what you are feeling. Here I am going to describe some of the experiences and insights you may receive as you go deeper into the space inside.

When I say 'going deeper', of course I am referring to the process of feeling it more and more and therefore being less separate from it. At this time you are likely to feel separate from everything, unless you have been, or are, practising feeling inside. It is actually the space that connects everything. As you can see around you, there is space everywhere. We are inclined to take the space for granted and focus on the objects, but clearly the objects are only possible because there is space. Otherwise there would be one blob here; but one blob of what? ...There would be no separation for anything to experience anything! So this is what has happened here. There is space which allows you to experience being separate, and the space is also the same intelligence that is creating the objects and indeed is your own space you feel inside. It is all the same. You have just forgotten it because you spend all your time focussing on the objects, either real here or in your own imagination. The more you begin to feel the space, the more you become the space and the more you become aware that the space is the nearest we can get to reality here. But what is it? That we cannot know, except to experience it as your own being behind all the forms. There are limits to the knowledge, even in Enlightenment. It is a little like waking up in a dream (whilst still asleep in bed) and knowing you are dreaming but being unable to wake up any more than that; and at the same time having no knowledge of the bed and the room your body is lying in. The only reality you know is that this is a dream, and you are dreaming it. You can see therefore it is your own mind that is creating everything, and yet it is still a dream and as such you cannot change things at will. You will however react to what happens in a less stressed way because you know it's not real anyway, and as such nothing can really hurt you. That is how Enlightenment is here! Ultimately there are no answers, beyond seeing clearer how things work.

The experience may begin with the feeling inside of peace, that in some way everything this moment is ok. You could probably think of all sorts of things that you need to do or that could be a problem, but at this moment, wherever you are sitting, for some reason everything seems ok. You will need to practice this as often as you can whatever you are doing. Practice feeling your breathing, your whole body right from your toes up your legs, into your body, arms and head, while seeing and hearing whatever is going on around you. You are at this time in your senses, which is the natural way to be. Then you let the body go, and just stay aware.

As you continue to do this over time, you may begin to see how life gives you little lessons. You will see someone say something or do something and will feel your emotions rise inside, and you will know that is why it happened; to disturb you! Yes, you can still react if you wish, but you will know what you are doing and why it happened. You will become increasingly responsible for your life and particularly what happens to you. You will blame others less for what they seem to do and how they make you feel, but you will also accept less blame for the irresponsibility of others, while at the same time becoming more aware of them and how they feel. The more you know yourself, the more you know others. Self-awareness is also awareness of others, though just as you will stop pandering to your own selfish emotional wants and judgements, you are equally likely to give less credence to the whinging and whining of others. You are growing up and becoming responsible, but only for what you think, say, feel and do; not for what others would like to put on you to avoid themselves accepting the same responsibility for their own life. And of course that's ok for them to do this. It is not their time and nothing can happen until it's time. You will just not take it into you; though you may still let them say it if you wish. But that will be your choice and you will learn as you grow, as you do in all things. A part of growing up is allowing children to be children, or the unconscious to remain unconscious as they wish.

As you go deeper and are reminded more often to 'wake up' and return from whatever little scene or scenario you were playing out in your head, you will enjoy the space more. It will never be easy to hold on to it for long as the drive for experience is so strong. What happens is the power within that 'wakes' you up does so more often, until it is there all the time. That is how Enlightenment is said to be effortless, if you have heard this. Clearly it can require effort for some time to hold the space as much and as long as you can. But the bit that wakes you up when you are unconscious is the bit that takes over when you have done it long enough, and that is when it becomes effortless; so stay with it.

You will see how life around you teaches you and gives and takes from you to teach you. Repeated amazing coincidences occur in your life, reaffirming that there is indeed some greater intelligence here than your own thinking and feeling mind. You will see that you are indeed a part of this intelligence, and as such you are not separate. This will soon become a knowledge that you will know without a doubt, as you feel and become the space more.

You will receive many insights of knowledge which are glimpses into how things are here. These are likely to pass, to be absorbed into you where they become a knowledge of truth. Then you know something. You may even get seemingly weird and crazy experiences which you would be reluctant to share or tell anyone for fear of being thought mad. Don't worry about these, and likewise do not try to repeat or hold onto them once they have gone. Frequently we only need an experience once to have what we need to learn. The normal way is to think an experience is the truth so spend the next 30 years (or whatever) trying to recreate the same experience, thus missing the rest of the journey beyond it. No experience is the truth. It is just an experience on the path to the truth. When the truth happens in you, it is the space before and behind any and all experiences, and as such is perhaps of 'no experience'. Holding onto something will only hold you back. Of course for you to do this, if you did, would be right too. There is no judgement here. We are just looking at how it is.

It is likely to be many months and/or years as you live in the world, growing in self-knowledge with each conscious experience. A lot of time may pass, or it may not, as you have glimpses into the space you are feeling ('you') and see this is indeed all there is. Your own being is creating everything here and you see you are alone in this dream world. This is likely to scare you. It is very rare to even see this, and it can be a terrifying experience. The fear is the attachment to experience, which is continuing to be dissolved as you practice feeling the space and thinking about the objects less and feeling less. Just keep going. The fear will pass.

Several years may pass (for the author it was 13 years after finding this teaching) and you may have long since given up asking if you are nearly there yet. You have worked so hard and had numerous insights, yet something still seems to be missing. You find you can reel off about Karma and Reincarnation (I will look at these later) and you know all about emotions and how they work. You may be the only person you know who is aware the space inside is creating this dream, and as such there is only one dreamer here. Your life is pretty good, but still has its problems (which you are dealing with well) and you do not know what else you can do to become Enlightened, but to carry on with what you are doing.

Then one day it may happen. You may be talking to someone (like the author was) or doing any number of activities, when suddenly something will change. You will be looking at your environment and suddenly it is you. It's ALL YOU! The walls, the ground, the trees, the cars, even the other people you are talking to, are all you. This is indeed one mind, one consciousness, and you are it. This is your dream and as such you are the beginning and the end of all that is. The space you are feeling, that you have always felt your entire life, is the only reality and nothing else is real.

The above may happen to you, or it may not. It doesn't matter. The point here is it cannot happen while you are looking for it, because to look for it is to look for an experience, which is to look past it. If you truly want it then you need to feel it now, by feeling the space inside you and see where you are and what you are feeling; and keep doing it. The more you do it, the more you do it.

Like all insights and experiences along the way, this too will pass. Nothing lasts here, even the experience of nothing; in fact especially the experience of nothing. It is only felt in the separation amongst the attachment to something. Over the following weeks and months this experience returns, slowly, though now there is no feeling in it at all. It seems to creep up unnoticed until you are so much in the space that there is no feeling as you become it consciously. After a while all you can announce is, 'I am this, whatever 'I' am?'

You are now 'Enlightened', listening to all these people around arguing and debating as to whether or not Enlightenment exists. And what it is if it does, and who is and who isn't? You hear them trying to decide who is from what they say or do and great Masters (Enlightened people) are discovered to have lied and cheated so are discounted. There are some people who, having had a flash of experience, 'run around' announcing they are Enlightened and trying to teach people what it is and how to do it. Your own life is now a constant unfolding of your own need for experience. It always was. But whereas previously it was troublesome and difficult at times, now it is easy and effortless. Each day, each moment is new, now. There is no holding on to the last or yearning for the next. Everything you need is right here right now, each and every moment. This is indeed your dream and you are the Master here. But Master of what? You are just a space that has realised it is creating a dream that all is separate, and as such even the experience of you will not last. As the need for the dream is satisfied it will become finer and finer, until it ends. But nothing is lost that was not here anyway. Just as when you awake from a dream at night, the dream is still within you and yet it never was real. However, this dream is a little different because it is indeed the dream of a lifetime. A dream where the dreamer is instantly lost amongst the forms, striving for more and more experience in its own world until, much later, begins to look for something more real. Eventually it feels within where there is no feeling but all is well and it begins the journey home to the place beyond the forms until there are no more forms; ...until next time.

Reincarnation

As one goes deeper into one's own being, which is now the only being, one comes to know more about life and how it works; about what is real and what isn't. There are a number of questions people like to ask when it comes to Enlightenment. One is regarding the idea of Reincarnation. Is it real?

To answer the question we need to be sure of what we are asking first. Are we asking 'is my body going to get up again and walk around after I am dead?' But this is probably not what we are asking, and it is extremely doubtful anyway. So, are we asking, 'after I am dead, will I come back into another body as some people say I have done before?' This is the most likely meaning of the question; so let's look at it. If you have indeed been 'here' before and you can't remember it, what good is it to you anyway? Whether this is your first life or twentieth or one hundredth, or indeed whether you have no more after this or one more or a hundred more, what good does it do you if you have no memory of them? It is just entertainment for the mind to think it has time and doesn't have to take responsibility now; 'I'll do it next time, or the one after, or the one after that'.

So, we can see, even if you do come back again (and we will look at this possibility), you will only have knowledge of the life you are living at the time (we will leave out past-life regression stuff for now, because this too only serves to give you the illusion of your continuing). And furthermore, the likelihood is you will have a different name, possibly a different sex, and some traditions even say you may be an animal of some sort. Are you getting the idea here? What good is any of this to you? You are here now, and we have established, if you ever did return, you will be a different person with a different name and a different memory, and possibly not even human... yippee. But at least you're back...Right? What an example of how we make a big issue out of nothing, with all these discussions of reincarnation and past lives.

So, what is the truth? Well, actually the above is almost it. The space inside you that you feel and are becoming more and more is the same space that will remain when you die. It has nowhere to go.

So you die and become more the space. As far as reincarnation goes, any attachment or need to experience which has not been satisfied creates another dream, and off it goes again. So is this you? Well, was the other one you? It's like you having a dream at night and dreaming you are called 'Roger'; the next night you dream you are called 'Bob'; and the next night you dream you are called 'Cathy'. So, who is a reincarnation of whom? Of course no-one is a reincarnation of anyone, because none of them were real. It was the mind creating them that was real, and not the characters it was creating

So, is reincarnation real? The space creating the dream remains, but it could hardly be said to 'incarnate' any more than you are 'incarnating' when asleep in your bed dreaming that you are somebody else. The attachment does indeed return, but I don't know if it could be said to 'belong' to any one of the characters. In fact it could be said to be the creator of the characters. So, 'No', there is no reincarnation; though death is not the end anymore than waking up is the end. You will go to sleep again and continue experiencing whatever it is you need to dream this time. Sweet dreams.

Heaven

Another little idea people have to give them something to look forward to and a reason or reward for all the pain and hardship they endure here, is paradise or Heaven. Let's look at this for a moment.

Let's assume all those people who worship in the way they have been told make it into the great place. Let's even say you do too. Great; what now? Are you 'you', or aren't you? What I mean is, do you still have all your memories, your resentments, all your thoughts and feelings about who you love and who you hate, what you like and what you don't; where you want to go and where you don't; who you will talk to and who you won't? Again, are you getting the idea? If there is a place called Heaven where all the 'chosen' people go who have worshipped in a certain way, unless they change, can you see we are just creating another place of suffering the same as down here? All the people are the same with all their emotions and attachments. Do you really want to go to a place called 'Heaven' where you suddenly wake up the same as you are now, surrounded by people who are also exactly the same as they were; except now they are even worse than before as now they are able to say 'See, I told you!' ...forever and ever and ever. You can't even commit suicide to get away from them (or from your-self, whether your 'self' is really 'you', or something separate) because, as we are told there is no death there, it could become a living Hell. (In fact do you see this? Whether it is Heaven or Hell is determined by your own emotional state that creates your own reality).

The only way this place 'Heaven' can have any reality of peace is for those who enter to have already been stripped of all their personal attachments, beliefs, opinions, likes, dislikes, regrets, fears, resentments, prejudices, hopes, wanting; in fact anything that makes you, 'you'. So, all we are left with is perhaps the space you feel inside, and some fading memories, without emotion, of past aspects of the dream and the last remaining remnants of the attachment to experience and separation before it ends totally.

It may be interesting also to have a look at the word the Buddhists use to represent the same idea, 'Nirvana'. I have been told this translates into ‘Nir’ meaning ‘No’, and ‘Vana’ meaning ‘Craving. Ie. ‘No Craving’. See the similarity? Except the Buddhists look for it while alive.

The truth is, anything that continues is still ‘something’, and as such is part of the ongoing dream. So, either Heaven is the end of the dream where all need to create another has been satisfied for now (so there is no dream, so no Heaven). Or it is a part of the dream which has yet to end. Either way, it is found in the space inside you, where you are complete and have all you need at this, and indeed any moment. Keep holding onto your awareness of where you are and of what you are feeling. That way you can indeed find Heaven on Earth (or Nirvana).

Free-Will

So is there 'free-will' or isn't there? We are told by some teachings there is only one consciousness here, one intelligence or being, and as such there cannot be 'free will' as there is only one will. (I suppose one could argue that perhaps at least the one intelligence is free as it is alone, but as it is experienced here as something separate from 'us', as something 'out there' or sitting above judging us then, if it has the only free-will, then clearly 'we' don't).

So, I will ask you, 'do you have free-will? Well, do you?' The experience is 'yes', I suggest. But let's have a look at what the term 'free-will' actually means.

We do not always have 'free choice' or 'free action' as we know. Examples include, can you choose now to walk into a hospital surgery and perform a brain transplant? More blatant examples would include, can you walk through the wall in front of you now? So we don't have 'free choice' or 'free action'.

What about 'free thought'? This is more subtle. Most of us may reply, 'Of course I have 'free thought'; I am thinking now'. Ok, but can you stop? Can you choose what to think about and when? Can you decide now what you will think about in 5 minutes? Can you always be sure to remember a birthday or an appointment, or where your car keys are? Can you even be sure to see the glaringly obvious solution to a problem, when it was there all the time? Can you say where an idea comes from, or why it doesn't to one person but does for the next? It is clear we do not have as much control over our thoughts as we like to think.

So, we are left with 'free-will'. The term, to me, means just that; the will to be free, or separate. And guess what? Here we are! You are reading this. The page is in front of you and if you look up and see another person, they are also separate from you; so clearly, whatever it is that wants to be separate, is. 'Free-will' is simply the attachment or need for experience that creates the forms of existence here to allow you to enjoy being separate, while you do. After a time of being separate, with all the pains, struggles and hardships you can endure, you may begin to wonder what it is all about and why you are here; in fact why any of this is here. That is when you begin to look inside, where you are aware of where you are and of what you are feeling, like now and, perhaps for the first time, really feel complete and whole. The will to be 'free' or separate is diminishing as you become more and more 'at one' with your own being, which is the source of all else. Even after 'Enlightenment', when you are aware of all this, the will to be separate or free still remains or the dream of being separate would no longer exist. It is just that you now know you are not really.

So, (to you reading this) you no longer need to worry about whether or not you have 'free-will'. You are separate so you do.

Karma

What is it? Some talk of karma when looking at past lives and repaying debts to those you have wronged and of others repaying their debts of past hurts they have inflicted on you. Let us have a look at what it really is, in our own language.

We have said the space you are feeling inside is the source of all that is here and it is the need for experience that creates the forms giving the apparent separation you see around you. We also know it is through living the dream that the very need for it is being dissolved and satisfied, until all need has been dissolved and the dream ends. Ok, so what is karma?

Karma is the name given to that same need for experience and attachment which keeps returning in similar circumstances until it has been satisfied. The circumstances will come up in your life, time and time again, giving you the same situation and thus raising the same emotions and feelings, until it is dealt with. Once done, there is no need for that situation to occur again, thus you are free of that piece of 'karma'. That is to say, the bit of attachment you were holding onto inside you, possibly unbeknown to you, was creating similar situations to allow you to relive them, over and over again, until you no longer want/need them. That is all karma is.

It is because we like to live the dream and give each person their own reality that we say we are repaying our debts to others, as they are to us; but in truth there is only your own space or being creating your own dream, allowing you to live and satisfy all need for experience. But as usual there is no problem here. Just continue to enjoy the dream, dissolving your emotion or karma as it comes up and stay as aware as you can of where you are and of what you are feeling, now and as often as you can.

There's No-body here!

Well that's what they say. 'There is no-body here. There is no-one to be, or not to be Enlightened. You are not reading this, and I did not write it!'

Great; now that's cleared that up..! But is it the truth? Feel inside you now. Are you here? Is anyone here?

Do you see how ridiculous it is? How it denies your own experience and therefore is of no help to you? If I am asked the question 'Is there anyone here?' I have to reply along the lines of 'There is something here, to even be aware of the question and to feel the space within where there is nothing. So, although I have to say I may feel nothing and am aware this 'nothing' is also everything, there is still something here that is able to look and see that there is nothing here'. That is to say, something is looking at the nothing. It could be said, 'then this is the 'nothing' looking at itself', and that may be so. But the 'nothing' is just a name given to the something, to represent the lack of something tangible.

Are you getting this? The teaching is really an attempt to explain what cannot be explained, in a way that cannot be understood. So, unless you are feeling it and have already realised it, I suggest it is of very little meaning to you.

Don't worry about it, and don't try to understand it. Don't even try to do it, because the same people who teach this say there is nothing to be done and no-one to do it anyway. They also say there is no teacher and no-one to teach, whilst they are (not) in front of an audience (not) teaching this, to no-one. I could say 'Good Luck', but there is no-one here to say 'Good luck' to the no-one there, so I'll save my breath that I haven't got in this body that isn't here that I am not feeling as I am not here to feel anything.

Already Enlightened!

Have you heard that one as well? 'You are already Enlightened, so there is nothing you can do or need to do. You are already there!'

Another not particularly helpful teaching, but in essence it means the same as the previous 'There is nobody here'. It won't answer any of your questions or help you deal with any of your problems or put to rest any of your many fears and worries and past regrets or hopes and wants. What it does is allows the un-enlightened to give up looking in the belief there is nowhere to go. In a sense this is absolutely true, if you are in the moment enough to realise the truth behind it. But until this occurs, you are still separate inside, and you know you are.

The confusion may come down to, as is often the case, the definition of the word 'Enlightenment'. It is true the space of Enlightenment is your true nature, and as such you are always 'That'. But do you know what 'That' means? If you take Enlightenment to also be the same as other names such as 'Self-Realisation' then you see that Enlightenment is just to realise your-self. It has never really meant anything else. But surely that means until you do realise it, you haven't, and as such are not Enlightened until you do. Sure, you are still the one being creating all that is here, but if you don't know that yet it seems a shame to pretend you do, or indeed be convinced that you can't.

This statement could also be suggesting the word 'Enlightenment' has no meaning! Ok, so let's have a look at that for a moment. You (let's say) are looking for Enlightenment and pay to see a person or buy their book who claims to know what Enlightenment is, only for them to tell you there is no such thing. Can you see again how ludicrous this is? You are paying money to a person who claims to know what Enlightenment is (who claims to be Enlightened, or how else would they know what it is), only for them to tell you it has no meaning. Perhaps you can explain to me what you have just paid for?

In the end it just comes down to different teachers and teachings, all doing their best to interpret and express the experience which is beyond understanding of the mind and with the limitation of words; and yet these words have to be interpreted back into an experience the listener (you) can understand. That is a long journey through mind and interpretation for something that has to be experienced but cannot be understood.

I can also acknowledge other's views on my own teaching. I am aware, for example, some may not like my using the term 'Dream' to describe what is going on here, for differing reasons (many because they aren't Enlightened, so haven't seen it yet). The Buddhists say 'Maya' meaning illusion, but I suggest it has more reality than that. The term 'Illusion' implies no reality at all, and yet this certainly has a reality, even if it is passing. My use of the term 'Dream' is because whatever characteristics you attribute to a dream, they apply here. Some may prefer I make it special by saying something like 'Eternal Dream' or 'Cosmic Dream', but the term dream still applies however the mind tries to flower it up to make it special.

Whichever way an Enlightened person describes the experience and whatever technique / or indeed lack of it, they describe to reach it (or even if there is nothing to reach by nobody here), in the end there should be a common thread in all Enlightened persons. In whatever terminology that is used I suggest it must always be a sense of peace or completeness and a lessening of the identification with 'I' or 'me' being separate. After that it comes down to the individual.

Enlightened = Not!

This is another little idea as to how to tell who is Enlightened and who isn't. Some expect an Enlightened person to shave their heads and wear orange robes, carry beads and a begging bowl. Some say Enlightened people have no need for money or nice clothes or a nice house. Many expect an Enlightened person to be celibate. Some still expect an Enlightened person to be able to perform miracles and walk on water, levitate and appear and disappear etc. There are even those who say a truly Enlightened person would cure the whole world's suffering, while others say you can't be Enlightened while alive. There are no doubt numerous other ideas, but there is one I find particularly amazing... 'You can't be Enlightened if you say you are!'

So, we have an experience which is impossible to understand and known only to the truly enlightened person who is in the living experience of being it. Everybody else (let's say) is looking for Enlightenment, and it is indeed very rare to find an Enlightened person; but some bright spark has come up with this idea that anyone who says they are, isn't! So what chance have you really got to hear first hand from an Enlightened person what it is? Clearly none at all, if you accept this; because as soon as you find a person who is, the moment they say they are, it means they are not; and yet if they say they are not, how do you expect to learn from them what it is? Again, do you see how crazy this idea is? In a way it is symbolic of the search for Enlightenment within yourself, in that, as soon as you find anything, that's not it, because Enlightenment is the source before anything is, so could be called 'non-experience'. But that does not help you in the search to find a person to teach you.

I suggest the idea may have come about because someone was jealous of an Enlightened person and saw the position as being superior, thus felt inferior. They then blamed the Enlightened person for making them feel this way. Of course it is perfectly possible the Enlightened person felt no such superiority and just offered to share the experience in which they found themselves, and happened to give it a name which is accepted 'Enlightenment'. (Having said that, it is also perfectly possible for an Enlightened person to intentionally make themselves out to be special. It's only their own dream after all; what have they got to lose?)

This idea also makes way for un-Enlightened teachers to imply the 'accolade' without actually having to be the genuine article, or admit they are not. Just by implying they are it whilst stating 'if they said they were it would mean they weren't' serves to increase the already mounting confusion.

So, to clear it up, I do indeed say I am Enlightened. But before anyone jumps in and says 'That means you are making yourself better than us, which is egotistical, so you can't be!' I will say there is no judgement in it for me. Is there for you? That is to say, I say I am Enlightened and offer to share what it is with those who wish to know, but I in no way say it is better to be than not to be. I just talk from this experience. Leave your own judgements behind if you can and just practice being aware of where you are and of what you are feeling. That is your own Enlightenment. Don't worry about anybody else's.

Why do I Teach?

Well, it's a fair question. Why do I teach, or indeed why do I do anything, if I know nothing's real and it's all a dream?

The answer is the same as why the dream is here in the first place. It is simply the need for experience, which equates to growing in self-knowledge and the living out of the attachment or need to have any experience at all. So I teach for me. In fact I do everything for me. Does that sound selfish? Do you really think you are so different? Are you so special, so separate, that you believe you do things for others and not for yourself? Again, let's have a look at this...

Putting aside for the moment that all is one and is created by the space within you and as such everything is done by (and indeed for) 'that', let's look at the basic act of giving. Why do you give? Do you give because it feels nice to give? See the question? If you give because it feels nice to give, then you are giving because it makes you feel nice. Is that not doing it for your self?!!

Ok, so you help someone. Do you help them because you feel good helping them? Do you see the same question?

Ok, another. Perhaps you give or help, not because you want to or it makes you feel nice or good, but because you feel you ought to? Ok, so you are doing it to satisfy your own feeling of obligation. Is that not doing it for your self?!

Perhaps you help or give because you are trying to achieve something or prove something or put on some sort of show or impression?! Perhaps you feel sorry for the person, and as such have to address your own feeling of sympathy? Do you see all you do is to address some need in you, whether conscious or otherwise? Is this sounding really depressing? Did you really think you were such a nice person that you were really doing everything you do, for others? Well, there is another side to this. As you accept you do everything for your self, because it suits you or because it feels right or even because you feel you have to, or whatever, what happens is you stop expecting anything back. Because you are doing it for you, you do not do it for thanks or gratitude or appreciation, or anything else (though, if you are doing it for money, then that is clearly another matter). You are aware you do everything and anything for you, because it is right for you to do that thing. If you get thanks, or appreciation, or anything else, that is great but, as that is not why you were doing it, it is not expected or needed. You also do not resent the person if they are not grateful or showing you 'enough' appreciation, though you may indeed not do it for them again.

So help or don't help. Give or don't give. But don't put your feelings of obligation or neediness for thanks or appreciation onto the person you have decided to help or give to. Grow up. This is your life. Don't give all responsibility to others for making you give or help, or whatever. You will only resent them anyway, which is certainly not loving them, and leaves you trying to convince yourself what you did was through love and therefore they should do this or say that to you through their own obligation to you. This is clearly selfish.

Again, be aware of where you are and of what you are feeling, and act from there. Sometimes you will feel it is right to help or give, while other times it won't be. Sometimes you will help or give through a feeling of obligation, only to feel afterwards you wasted your time. Other times you may help or give because you wanted to get something, again to find you wasted your time. The more you do what feels right to you, with no expectations of getting anything and not putting any feeling of obligations onto the person you are helping, the easier giving becomes. Give or don't give. Just do it because it is right for you. That is its own reward.

The Spiritual Life

You may have noticed, if you have been looking into Enlightenment and what it is for some time, I have so far not mentioned words 'spirit' or 'spiritual'. Why is this? These words are usually very important to people looking for some greater truth, and I claim to be Enlightened and am able to talk as if I know what I am talking about and yet I do not use these words; why? It is because they mislead and there is no need. In themselves the words do not mislead, because they are just words, but the meaning we put to them is something other than the truth.

Let's try it. What does the word 'spiritual' suggest to you? For most the word conjures up all sorts of ideas and practises, none of which I do, and therefore I do not claim to be spiritual; I am just Enlightened (or, as the Buddha is recorded to have said. "I am awake"). So what is the difference? Well, you have seen the difference. The experience of Enlightenment is just of realising what you are (or perhaps what you are not). You can be Enlightened whoever you are, wherever you are and whatever you do. It is just waking up to who you really are behind what you think you are.

The 'Spiritual Life' as it is commonly understood is also the pursuance of the realisation of what 'I' really am, but often involving particular practises, exercises, traditions or teachings. An Enlightened person comes to see it really doesn't matter what they do. That is where you get the teachings from, that there is nothing you can do as you are already there. If there is indeed a 'Spiritual Life' it is your whole life, and not just from the time you begin chanting, ringing bells, listening to whale music or sticking your toes in your ears.

So do what you do, and be aware of where you are and of what you are feeling while you are doing it. This is your Spiritual Life, whatever it is you are doing.

"Be aware of where you are
And of what you are feeling"

Chapter 4

Can Animals become Enlightened?

...Fair question. If humans can, can animals, and what would it be like if they were?

Firstly, as your own personal experience deepens in you, you will begin to see (and later perhaps even realise) the space within you is the one being, the one consciousness creating everything, and as such 'you' are the only one here. So whatever I say about animals, or indeed anyone being or not being Enlightened, Nick Roach included, none of it is real as you are the only one who can truly realise it. The rest of us will of course be here while you need us (don't try to work that out or understand it. You will see it when it is time).

If Enlightenment is of living in the moment, in the now, then it could be said animals are already Enlightened. However, the other side of Enlightenment is, of course, all the knowledge that comes with it as to what is, or isn't, real. Animals do not have the ability to access this part of the knowledge and as such, even within this dream, they are unable to realise it is only a dream (unlike everybody else around you). They act simply on experience and intuition. Some are indeed very clever, but (as far as we can see) it takes the human brain with its reflective capacity to realise itself; to experience the knowledge 'I am this', 'I am all there is'.

That said, it doesn't really matter who is or isn't. The point is, are you conscious now, aware of where you are and what you are feeling? Because if you are, that is the nearest you can come to reality, to the truth, to Enlightenment. If you are not, then it doesn't help you if the whole world is Enlightened except you. You are what matters; your own truth you feel within where you are complete and whole and at peace. Be The Truth and live The Truth; stop looking for it outside of you!

Being Creative

How can you be creative while living in the moment?

In a sense you are always living in the moment. You can't be 'any-when' else. What you mean is, 'How can you be creative if you are aware of where you are and of what you are feeling?' Do you see there is actually no question? Why should being aware of where you are and of what you are feeling have any detrimental effect on creativity? In fact many would say, it is in the moment where there is absence of thought when inspiration occurs. Thinking and worrying about problems is not a great technique to induce creativity of any kind.

In Truth 'Creativity' comes from the space within you that I am getting you to feel. That is where all 'genius' comes from; where all ideas emerge from that are 'out of the blue' and seem to be given from 'Heaven'. So, the more you are able to remain in this place now, the more you are likely to receive inspiration and great ideas and intuition. I am here now, in the space. It is constant for me, which is one of the characteristics of Enlightenment and is how I am able to talk of these things and write this book. My mind has not worked all this out and I have not learnt it from someone else. To the extent you are able to get your thinking mind and feelings out of the equation, by being aware of where you are and of what you are feeling, like now, the simpler and clearer life becomes; including seeing solutions to problems and being creative. So stay with it. It is only 'you' anyway, what have you got to lose?

Dangerous Sports

So what is the attraction of dangerous sports? It is true they can be exciting and exhilarating and thus feed the emotions, but there is a point beyond these feelings that some sports take you to; where your very life is at risk each and every moment and, were you to lose your focus, you would face almost certain death. What is happening here? You may have read enough of this book to be able to answer this already, but I'll take you through it.

We spend the vast majority of our lives in our imagination with our feelings of like and dislike, hope and fear and regret, and we sometimes look for some peace. So what appeal would life-endangering sports have, beyond taking your mind off your problems? Well actually that's the truth, but it goes deeper than that. We have seen, or are beginning to see, to be aware of where you are and of what you are feeling can put you in a place of completeness and peace. Here you are doing it consciously and in your own time; but what if you didn't know about this? What if you wanted to find the moment now where you are at peace and didn't know where to look? Well, one place to look is at anything which forces you to be in the moment, be it solo-climbing with only the finger tips of one hand preventing you from falling to your death as you dangle from a rock face, or surfing waves the size of office blocks where a fall is likely to be your last, or overtaking another car on a bend at speeds so fast you can barely hold the steering wheel, or any number of other dangerous activities which require your full attention. When you put your full attention into anything, you are at peace. The problem with this method is when you stop. You are likely to find you become addicted to the experience (as it is your own being after all) and will not know another way to find the same sense of peace and completeness. Now you do. You may still do all those things if you are moved to, but now you do them through conscious choice and not through a yearning for some sense of peace which you can find nowhere else. Stay with it; it does get easier (even if it doesn't always seem like it).

Drugs

So what do drugs do? Is that a silly question? Perhaps everyone knows what they do. Of course most think whatever drugs they take are acceptable while the others aren't. Such as smokers say is ok to smoke, but may not take other drugs. People who drink alcohol will often remark how awful drugs are, not wishing to notice the glass of wine or beer they are holding at the time, or even the cigarette in the mouth. People who take drugs such as speed or ecstasy may say how awful cocaine is, and people who take cocaine may say how awful Heroin is. People who do all these illegal drugs but don't drink alcohol may point out the huge number of deaths each year which result from alcohol related incidents and the infinitely more families that are ruined as a result of addiction to it. So what is going on?

You know by now what is going on, don't you?! Everybody is just looking for an escape from the mental and emotional torture their mind and emotions put them through daily. This could be simply coping with stress and problems in their daily life at work or within the family, or often as younger people looking for some excitement to fill the gap they are feeling within themselves. All searching and trying is really trying to get to the same place; to a sense of peace and fulfilment which is available to you at any moment, if only you would practice being aware of where you are and of what you are feeling.

So take drugs if you must, but whatever experiences you have do not last. That is why you have to keep taking them. They do not solve the problems or do you any favours at all. It is true alcohol numbs the senses in some way so may help you to relax. You are also slower to respond and less alert and even further away from your Enlightenment than normal. That is why you claim sometimes you did not know what you were doing when you were drunk. You were not fully 'here' or in control.

Then there are the drugs that give sensations and experiences other than just numbing the senses to avoid facing life or yourself. These are the ones that give a 'high' and even seem to offer insights and experiences into greater realities and alter one's sense of perception. Here you are totally aware you are still you, but the world around you has changed (instead of you being drunk and the world being the same). Again the high must come down, so nothing has really changed, but I suggest the high is only in contrast to your normal state of experience. The more you are able to practice simply being aware of where you are and of what you are feeling, your need for these drugs, or indeed any sort of recreational or avoidance drugs, will diminish. I also suggest you may begin to find some of the insights you were having on the drugs, which you took to be just amazing gibberish, had more reality than you gave credence to. But now you will become your own truth which is not reliant on a pill, a snort or a shot in the arm to give you the knowledge or sense of peace. Again, stay with it. As has been said, 'The Truth is within you'.

Who am I? Who are you?

I am not asking you to tell me my name or yours. I wish us to look at the meaning of the questions. So, Who am I?

'I' am the space you are feeling inside, when you are aware of where you are and of what you are feeling. Here there are no opposites and, as we now know, there is only one. It is perhaps interesting therefore that the letter 'I' is so similar to the figure '1'. So, when you ask 'Who am I? The first answer is, 'I am the space 'I' feel within where there is no feeling'. It is only in this world of separation that it is possible to reflect on one's own being (of nothing), so certainly 'I' am reliant on this to 'be' at all.

So, 'Who are you?' It can be seen that 'you' has an opposite here, 'me'. Both only exist in form. 'Me' is what one's own body, mind and feelings are called as a unit, and 'you' is the name given to all the others. (This may seem confusing, but people do like to ask this question, so bear with me. In truth this description serves no purpose other than to answer the question).

To finish off simply (as much as possible), 'I' am the space inside where there is no feeling. 'Me' is what I call 'my 'self'' in this existence and 'you' is what I call all the other bodily forms. 'My-self' is not 'me'. It is my identification with being 'me', with being separate. So, before you ever ask this question again 'Who am I?' just feel the space inside you, and that's it. Where else could it be? Did you really think you would have to go off round the world to find your-self? (It's almost funny, isn't it?) And you clearly don't need a Counsellor, Therapist or Psychologist to answer your question 'Who am I?' (In fact, after reading this book you may know more than they do). Just stay aware of where you are and of what you are feeling. That's your truth.

Where are you?

Either now or any other moment come to that! Where should you be, and what should you be doing?

Do you understand the question? Are you often doing one thing while thinking you should be doing something else, or wondering if you are doing the right thing, or even just quite happily doing whatever you are doing while imagining doing something else? No wonder you don't know who you are or what it is all about, if you spend so much time imagining being somewhere else! What did you expect?

Now's the time to start growing up! This is when you have the opportunity to change your whole life just by being honest, with no-one else but you. You are here. Your body is here. There is no need to imagine being somewhere else! Sure, if you need to, for a few seconds, remember where your car is, but we both know that is not what we are talking about here. We are talking about the lack of honesty where you spend the majority of your life trying to be in two places at once.

This is what I mean by 'be aware of where you are and of what you are feeling'. I mean just that. Stop the idle film show that goes on and on and round and round and over and over the same old stuff, getting nowhere but separating you from the truth of who and what you are; from your Enlightenment. Your attention can only be in one place at a time so, while you are thinking and lost in your imagination, that is what you are; lost. Enlightenment, in the sense of 'Self-Realisation', means just what it says. How did you ever hope to find out anything about your-self, anything about what is real and what isn't, if you can't even be aware of where you are and of what you are feeling.

So, start now, and keep doing it! The answers will come.

Doing the Right Thing

Having established you should (if this is right for you) be aware of where you are and of what you are feeling, what if you do think you should be somewhere else? What if you are sitting somewhere and your mind is driving you mad about going somewhere or doing something else? Simple answer: GO AND DO IT! What is the problem?

You see, this is all about being honest with what is going on inside. If there is something you clearly cannot do or somewhere you cannot go, then of course you must accept the fact. Thinking about it does not make it so and just separates you from the feeling of being complete and thus you feel incomplete, increasing the yearning and perpetuating it.

So, what to do? Just be as honest as you can. Your only job (if I may say so) is to be free of the discomfort and remain conscious. If you think you should be doing something else or be somewhere else, and it is really not letting you rest, you will need to take some action. If you cannot go there nor do it, you may need to make a phone call to someone, or at least take whatever action you feel can be made in the right direction, so you are able to know you have done all you can. Once done, let it go. You are likely, as usual with any problem or disturbance, to feel the pressure to make you go into the imagination and relive and feed the emotion over and over again; but don't. To the extent you are able to resist this and remain as conscious as you can, of where you are and of what you are feeling, you will return to the space inside where you are complete and at peace. Action will set you free. The mind likes to think about things without doing anything about them. It likes to be dishonest and whinge and whine and think about things it will not, or cannot change. You are realising a greater truth than your thinking and feeling merry-go-round. Just stay aware. You are already it.

There are No Answers

What does this mean? ...It means just that! When you get to the end of all the answers, you find there aren't any.

So where is the end of the answers? It is when you truly realise 'I am this' and know your own being, whatever it is, is the source of all things and each and every moment you are aware all you see and experience is your own creation. Ok, but what then? Nothing, that's what; you just live it.

The explanation behind it is this: This is an intelligence or mind living in its own dream. You are able to 'wake up' here and realise 'you' are dreaming this and that even your own sense of being only exists in this dream world. But that is as far as the knowledge goes. No matter how far you push, how deep you dig, dive, burrow or shoot into the apparent solar system, it is all within this dream. And no matter what you seem to realise, that too is within this dream. Your reality, even once you realise this is a dream, does not change; you just know it's no longer real, at least not in the sense you always thought. It is real in the sense that it is here now, and should you stub your toe, have chronic tooth-ache or something more horrific, yes it hurts. So you would state this is certainly real. However, as far as you are concerned at the time when you are asleep in your bed at night dreaming, that is real too, while it is there. Your whole experience of what is real or what isn't is provided through your senses, which are from your brain. We have seen how hypnotists can alter a person's sense of reality while still awake. We go for major operations and feel nothing when under anaesthetic and our senses are altered through being blind, deaf or paralysed. Can we really be so sure of what our senses tell us is real? It is after all, as far as we are taught, just electrical impulses being translated by the brain (and you will realise even this is only dreamt). So, enjoy being here as much as you are able. Practise being as aware as you can, of where you are and of what you are feeling, and wake up – if it is right for you to do so. But the faster you can stop searching and questioning, the easier it will be; because in the end, there really are no answers. There is only this.

I don't know what came over me!

You have heard this before; this and other sayings such as 'I was beside myself with anger' and 'I didn't know what I was saying'. What do these sayings mean? Well, you know now.

What has happened is clearly the person, you, has allowed the emotion to take control. You were not conscious of where you are and of what you are feeling and the emotion took over. In fact it always does. It is rare for you to be aware of where you are and of what you are feeling for any length of time, as we know. That is what this book is about. You spend so much time in your imagination, allowing the emotion, which behaves like a living entity, to say and do what it likes. You haven't really looked at it before, but it needs to stop. You need (if you are going to become a mature adult, responsible for your own thoughts and feelings) to practice truly living in your senses.

Anytime you wake up now, and see you were not aware and were unconscious, you may begin to notice the actions the emotions perform with your body. What you say and do out of unconscious 'habit'. Are there phrases you always say but have never noticed or questioned why? Are there things you do or say or think about which have always been there but you do not know why? Do you repeat phrases such as 'You know' and 'Know what I mean?' and 'sort of like' and any phrase which takes up space and energy but serves no purpose but for the announcement that you are not present? You might act a certain way, stand a certain way, pull a certain face, again anything you often do but have never really noticed. The more you can make all your words, thoughts and deeds conscious, the less any emotion will be able to dive in to act through you. The down side of this will be that never again will you be able to blame the emotion for anything you think say or do. It will all be you, and you will accept this. And why shouldn't you? As you were fully conscious and aware at the time when it was said or done, it means you were in touch with the space within, where all is well and you are complete. You have no fear, no worries, nothing to defend, no-one to blame and nothing to want. You are just being as straight as you can be and doing what you do, and being conscious and aware as you do it. That is the most you can ever do. Just stay with it. You are beginning to work with life, not against it.

"Be aware of where you are
And of what you are feeling"

Chapter 5

Religions

'Never talk about politics or Religion' they say. And that is because of the strong feelings that can arise when discussing these subjects. But aren't Religions supposed to be teaching of God and 'love thy neighbour' and 'Judge not, lest ye be judged', or even just focussing within and feeling the oneness with all life? Where does all this strong feeling come from?

From what I can see, the main Religions are focussed around one man who teaches of God. I would suggest this man, whichever one, was probably Enlightened, and thus able to talk of the truth and about various aspects of life in whichever country and time the man was in. Whether or not we accept Jesus existed or whether it was a revision of the old pagan myths, the stories teach 'Be still and know that I am God' and 'I and my Father are One' and similar phrases. Buddhism, or the little I know of it, teaches of going within where the experience of 'nothing arising' is felt; where the mind is still and has no desires (wants) and the knowledge is present of the cycle of birth and death, and many aspects of how things work here.

When the Enlightened man/teacher dies, what happens to the followers? Either another Enlightened person begins his own 'school' from his own experience and teaches his own teaching, or the remaining followers of the previous Master have only the words he left behind to teach them; thus these words become a tradition or religion, perpetuated by the 'wannabe' priests who haven't done it for themselves so teach what someone else said, interpreting the old Master's words in ways that suit their own needs. Then other priests, who do not agree with some of the interpretations, split off to make their own church with their own slant on what the Master had said. This now conflicts with the interpretations of the words of another former Master and the two churches argue and fight over which one is correct. How ridiculous, when it is all about realising the truth within your own being anyway, to realise what you really are.

So you don't need to follow any religion or indeed anyone at all. I am even telling you not to follow Nick Roach, but instead take what is true for you, which then becomes yours. It is all your own knowledge anyway. I cannot give you anything except for reflecting back to you what you already are. If someone's words are true for you, then live the words, but do not follow the man. You do not need to follow anyone any longer. You are the truth; the space inside where you are aware, of where you are and of what you are feeling, is the only truth. Feel it, live it, be it!

Meditation, Tai Chi & Yoga

What do they do? What is the point in sitting by candle light chanting for hours on end, with whale music playing and your toes stuck in your ears; or moving really slowly in practiced moves handed down through millennia, repeating the same actions over and over again, day after day, week after week, month after month, year after year, for tens of years? Does it really do any good at all? What is the point?

Bottom line..? The point is (as usual) to become conscious of where you are and of what you are feeling. What else would it be? It is true there could be a possibility that stretching and such movements could help physical health in some way, but that is not the ultimate aim. The ultimate is always to reach Enlightenment; in fact 'Yoga' means 'union', but union with what? Of course there is no 'what' or there could be no union. Union means Union. There is only one. So the purpose of all these practises is to work towards Enlightenment; towards Self-Realisation.

The problem is the practitioners have not learnt how to bring it into their daily lives. The normal way is to sit down for an hour or so at a time, often much longer, concentrating as hard as you can or going into a trance like state where you feel relaxed, then getting up and forgetting about it for the rest for the day; until sitting down to do it again later. By all means do whatever you wish to do. Stretch, run, walk, cycle, chant, or levitate, but the point as always is to be as aware as you can be, of where you are and of what you are feeling. And I don't mean just while you are doing it, but when you get up to walk across the room to make a cup of tea; when you get changed, get in the car to drive home or to work, when you are sitting watching television or talking to others. This could perhaps then be referred to as meditation all day, but I just say it is being conscious. So, do whatever you are moved to do; just be awake while you do it.

You can't Handle The Truth!

Can you? Do you know what the truth is yet? If you don't, that's ok. You aren't actually supposed to. I am aware in writing this book I am offering something nobody wants. Not because they don't want an end to their struggles and problems, but because nobody wants the dream to end. To see this is only a dream and all is 'my' own creation (yours) is pretty final at the time. Yes, the dream of living continues and you do get used to it and it becomes lighter and easier. But what if you don't want to wake up yet? What if you are enjoying the ups and downs and identification with what is going on here?

I can see, to you, I am just like the person who spoils the magician's tricks by telling you how they are done, or perhaps worse, the kid who tells the other kids that there is no Father Christmas. We know the magician's tricks are just tricks, but we love to be amazed as to how they work. However, the child does not even know Father Christmas is not real and, although has not actually seen him flying across the sky with reindeer or teleporting his way up and down chimneys, and even though it defies all the child is learning about what is real and what isn't, there is the love of the fantastic and mystical and it isn't questioned. As soon as it is pointed out, it does not take long for the truth to dawn in the child.

So, should I even be writing this book at all? Perhaps I should just withdraw from the world or keep my head down and get on with my 9-5 job, paying the bills and enjoying my own life; not worrying about all those so deep in the dream that they feel, and proclaim at times, this is a living nightmare. And yes it is a nightmare, for those who feel trapped.

The truth is, I do not know whether it is 'right' to teach this or not, but I do know it cannot do any harm. Why not? Simply because no harm can be done here! This is your dream, and I am telling you that. The worst that can happen is you begin to see it and wake up. You may even begin to enjoy this and see life unfolding before you like a red carpet, with all your dreams laid out and being offered, one after the other. And why shouldn't this happen? This is your dream after all. Why shouldn't you have what you want? The trouble is you need to learn not to be identified with the comings and goings here in order to really enjoy it and have what you want. While you try to fight and go against the tide, it will be tough and you won't go far. Of course, that is the game. ...Go where? There is nowhere to go. You are here creating this book to read and, like any dream, when you get up to move around the forms move around giving the sense of you moving, like a simulator. You can either continue to identify with the shapes in front of you, or feel inside the vehicle where you are and where the truth is, where all is well each and every moment. Whether you see it or not or whether you become Enlightened in the next 10 minutes, 10 years or never, does not matter. The space inside you will always be the space inside you. That is the truth and it cannot leave you. You may have left it, or so it appears, but it never really goes anywhere.

So don't try to become Enlightened. Don't try to do anything (unless you do). Do whatever you are moved to do and if it seems right to you, but practice being aware of where you are and of what you are feeling. If you have any 'job' here at all, any 'higher' purpose, that is it. But to attain and achieve this and to wake up only brings the end of the dream that bit closer, so I cannot tell you really that you should do it. The dream is here to be enjoyed, in whatever form. Enjoy your dream. It is tailor made for you, by you.

What happened when Nick Roach Realised this?

First I had a feeling of completeness when aware of the space inside, as I direct you to do. As time passed and I practised this more and more, facing and dissolving more emotion (the need to be separate) I came to see there really is an intelligence of some sort behind this existence and witnessed amazing coincidences occurring time and time again.

After a while I began to see there is indeed one intelligence here and I am a part of it, and later this changed to 'I am it'! ...And why not? It's obvious, isn't it? If there is one intelligence or God or Cosmic-Consciousness or whatever, then the space inside one's body must be it! Time passed and I came to see this space I am feeling is creating everything around me each and every moment, and as such 'I' am all alone here. This was very frightening and the first time I saw it I sat and cried, then talked myself out of it and forgot it. Perhaps two or three years passed before it came to me again, this time I was ready for it and saw it to be true. Though I was ready, it was still tough and I spent three days in my dressing-gown sitting at home not seeing the point in even getting dressed. What is the point if nothing's real and it's all a dream? (It may be interesting to know 'Life' had so happened to have already arranged for me to have these three days off work).

Having spent these days at home, doing little else but sitting on the sofa looking at the four walls, totally shocked and feeling trapped in hell at the prospect of having to spend another 60 or 70 years in this nightmare of a dream where I am the only one here, I was given a few words from the depth of the silence within me...

"...A Dream it may be,
But the Dream goes on!"

Nick Roach 1994

...With that I saw, real or not, this must be lived. I got up, got dressed and went to work.

So, whether you see this is a dream or not, whether you are so ingrained in this existence that the sheer idea of the being a dream repulses you, or indeed if you have already had insights into the nature of things here, nothing really changes. This still must be lived. What changes is the fighting stops when you realise you are creating it all anyway. Until then it is one long battle, one enemy after another, one situation or heartache after another; but that's ok too. This is your life, your dream; you can have what you want. You can get stuck in or sit back and watch. Either way, it's yours to enjoy. You cannot lose and there is no failure here. There's no reason why you should be Enlightened, and some may say there is little reason as to why you would even want to be. But if you do want it, you know now where it is. Just be aware of where you are and of what you are feeling, and keep doing it.

Miracles

You have heard about these old Eastern Gurus levitating, walking through walls, appearing and disappearing and producing items from mid air. Does or did this really happen, and if so, how?

Well, in theory anything is possible. It is true usually certain rules are adhered to here, so we have come to accept some things as normal and even possible, and not others. But as we don't really know how this all works, our beliefs are just that, beliefs; and as such we don't really know very much at all. As you come to see this is a dream, with all the possibilities that accompany this description, you come to see indeed anything is possible. That is not to say it will happen, but it could. Don't get too hung up on the idea of miracles etc. If they occur, ok, but so what? How does it help you in your life if a chap claims to perform miracles? Let's say you do put credence to the claims and later they are exposed as sleight of hand trickery. Again what difference does it make to you? This is your life and indeed you are entitled to enjoy and explore as you wish, but if you are unconsciously searching outside of yourself for some truth, you will be misled, let down or disappointed, because the only truth is within you; your own being you feel as the space or knowledge 'I am'. The miracle is truly the entire existence here, be it an insect, a sports car, a chap walking through a wall, or simply your own body. Don't make anybody special. Live your own truth which is where you are aware of where you are and of what you are feeling, now. You are it. Feel it, be it.

Midas Touch

It occurred to me I may have 'whet your appetite' a little with regards to even the possibility of performing miracles, so let's have a look at what it would be like if you could.

You may recall the story of King Midas who wished whatever he touched would turn to gold. When he got his wish it almost killed him as he couldn't eat anything. Let's say you at any moment could have whatever you wanted. You want to be on holiday and suddenly, barely have you finished the thought before you find yourself sitting on a beach with the sun blazing down, holding a cold drink and watching the waves... lovely. Are you alone here? Let's say you mentioned it to a friend and now you are both here. Perfect.

Then one of you suggests it would be good to be in the water and suddenly you are waist high in the water. Ok, this is good, but it may have been fun to walk down the beach, would it not? You feel the sun burning your shoulders and it becomes uncomfortable. As fast as you notice it, the heat subsides. No need to get into the shade for you. You suggest to your friend it may be nice to go to the club later, and your friend agrees. At that moment there you both are, standing outside a club several hours later. There is a queue. No problem, suddenly you are sitting inside at a table with drinks.

You want to take a sip of your glass and before you know it your glass is at your lips; but this time there is no need to drink. You have already imagined the liquid going down to your stomach; in fact you have imagined the feeling of even being thirsty has already gone. Now your life really changes. You can have whatever you want, the moment you want it, but therefore you do not want anything. Nothing has to happen because your wants are satisfied purely by wanting them to be satisfied. You do not need to eat, drink, go to work, pay your bills, sleep, walk, talk, in fact you don't have a body because you have no need of one anymore. You are just a space of pure intelligence where there is nothing to want and nothing ever happens because you are complete.

Does that sound pretty boring? Can you see what would happen if you were able to perform miracles and have whatever you want just by wanting it, with no time or effort required to attain it? That is the fun here. That is the dream. It is true this is your own dream, but that does not mean you can have whatever you want, or think you want, as soon as you want it; as that would spoil the dream. The dream is, you can't! You are allowed to want something and then must wait for it to come to you. That is the play. Just enjoy the waiting and the trying too if you do, but this must be done here. There is no escape. And what is there to escape from? Just time between events, and yet time is the one thing that is running out in this world of time, as the dream must end. Just stay with it. You will always get what you need to experience, even if it is of wanting what you can't have. All is part of the game of life.

Enlightenment in the West

We have heard and read perhaps many stories about Eastern Masters with their wonderful poetic words and phrases and meaningful anecdotes which are great to read and listen to. We are often fascinated by their talk of being 'desireless' in the moment now and wanting for nothing but what is here now. They are timeless and infinite and beyond the cycle of birth and death. Some are said to even have done miracles and the world's great religions are based around these 'God Men' of the East. So how does the Enlightenment of those days compare with the Enlightenment I speak of here?

If you read the above carefully you may have noticed there is actually no difference. From the living in the moment where there is no time and wanting for nothing, to the need to exist having been satisfied so there is no longer any need to create another dream (until a new need occurs, but that's another story), the experience is the same. Of course how could it be different? If an individual is truly able to realise the point before anything exists, where there is no time and the experience is infinite, whether it is realised now, last century or in one thousand centuries from now, the experience must be the same. There is nothing to change because the individual (you) are experiencing the ultimate truth beyond all forms and shapes and goings on here. There is indeed nothing to do and nowhere to go, beyond satisfying whatever needs that are responsible for creating this. You have the ultimate truth within you. Do not put it onto someone else, no matter how important you believe them to be. The truth is within. Just be it.

"Be aware of where you are
And of what you are feeling"

Chapter 6

Can an Enlightened person be ill?

Of course, if it is right. By that I mean there is no judgement saying it should not happen if it does. However, because the Enlightened person is likely to be less emotional about situations, they may heal quicker and suffer less than another person might.

That said, there are also wonderful medicines, both scientific and 'natural', which would appear to work miracles. An Enlightened person may well have knowledge of cures of herbs and similar remedies, but also he might not; just as another person may have knowledge of these herbs, and the next may not. Being Enlightened does not mean you never get ill, neither does it mean you know all there is to know about everything (I have been asked, if I am indeed Enlightened, can I tell the person how many tiles are on their bathroom wall?). It simply means you have seen through the illusion here and are in constant touch with the truth behind, where you are complete and all is well. You can still feel pain, hunger, tiredness and are subject to all the usual goings on here. However, you are likely to be moved by them emotionally much less as you are aware this is a dream, while also being aware it must be lived. There is no escape really. And again I ask, escape from what? This is just the intelligence (you) enjoying your own dream. If you are finding it tough, perhaps you are 'too' identified with it.

Let's put this in perspective. I imagine the majority of the people reading this are pretty able-bodied and have full ability to walk around (If you do not, that in no way prevents you from becoming Enlightened). I have heard it said on occasions that some do not believe they would be able to go on if they were to become paralysed; that life would not be worth living (I am not going to go into how insulting this is for a person in this predicament learning to live with it).

Let's imagine you are paralysed and have the choice. You can end it now; leave everything behind. Everything you love and everything you enjoy, all the birds, the flowers, the grass, the trees, the water, the people smiling and talking to you, everything here that this dream provides. True you cannot get up and run around if you are paralysed. Perhaps you cannot even scratch you own nose. But there are people who love you and care for you in every way they can and, what is more, you are Enlightened. You are aware this is your dream, your creation and here you are watching all the goings on and enjoying the experience of being separate from all these other shapes and forms around you. You have lost nothing. You are complete and you are loved, and you love. You are aware, should the dream end, it all ends. You are still you at that moment, but with no dream to experience, there would be no experiences at all and, paralysed or not, there is still much to experience here.

So, always do what you can to be as well as you can be. Some take medication while others refuse. Some take alternative therapies while others refuse. Some will take strenuous exercise while others do none. The Enlightened person may do any of these or others, or none of these, like anyone else. The difference is the experience and state of mind and being they are in, while they are doing it. I suggest you at least practice being aware of where you are and of what you are feeling. That is the greatest medicine you can take for the human condition here, whatever your own condition is. From then on you simply do what feels right.

How does being Enlightened affect memory?

There are two ways this can go. The first is, as you are more conscious and more alert and aware, you are likely to remember more and learn quicker. However, the other side is you can become less identified with things which many would say are important, such as birthdays and anniversaries (though chaps are known to be pretty useless at this area anyway, so no change there). With regards to the latter, the consequences of this are lessened though because, as you become more Enlightened, you begin to appreciate what you have more and more each day. Therefore people may not look for you to compensate for not loving them the rest of the year by buying flowers on their birthday or anniversary, as everyday with you will feel like their birthday or anniversary. But not because you are anything special, though they may express their feelings for you that you are; it is only because you love, acknowledge and appreciate them all day everyday.

With regards to remembering other day to day stuff, what is likely to happen is you will begin to learn what you will and will not remember, and what steps to take to ensure all that needs to be remembered, is. This may be through leaving a note stuck to the front door, or leaving your keys, money and mobile phone altogether, or phoning home to leave a message on your own answer-phone to remind you to do something. Practises such as these mean you don't actually need to worry about whether or not you will remember something. You are responsible enough to ensure in advance you cannot forget it. The memory is totally unreliable and yet, within this unreliability, you will see at any moment a flash of memory can give you something really important that you didn't even know you needed to remember. Memory comes and goes. You, the space inside, are constant. Just be aware of where you are and of what you are feeling, and take whatever action you need to.

Something I will mention, while memory is unreliable, I do find those memories that do come to me are pretty clear. Of course I may not recall them at all, but because I was conscious at the time and am again when need to recall them, when they do come there is no emotion to get in the way to twist, interpret or pervert those memories; and thus they, when they are there, are pretty reliable. It seems usual for most to have many partial memories of events, remembering only what they want to remember, such as 'I said this and you said that', when what really happened was totally different. They were just too emotional and unconscious at the time to be aware of what they were saying, and too emotional and unconscious now to see it. So once again, you are seeing it's always best to be aware of where you are and of what you are feeling, as much as you can. Stay with it; it does get easier.

Can Children be Enlightened?

If you take Enlightenment to be living in the moment with little or no identification with the forms and shapes of this existence, then babies are born Enlightened. That is to say, they are still pretty well in touch with the one consciousness and experience of no separation. It is the process of living amongst the shapes and separation that induces identification with the body, ie 'That is over there, so 'I' am over here...? Oh, yes, here I am!'

So the child learns it is the body and struggles to do what is best to give the body what it feels it needs to be complete and whole, having forgotten the feeling of being complete and whole is already within it. It is really tough as time and time again what it thought it needed in order to feel whole again is denied it. Each time that it gets what it wants, it is not long before the yearning starts again. It does this because the feeling of being complete (as you feel now within) has no feeling on its own. It can only be experienced in any way against the contrast of the separation. Feel complete for more than a few minutes and the mind is yearning for more experience. It yearns to feel complete and then yearns to feel something (which means to be separate again), and the process is an ongoing cycle of seeking fulfilment amongst the imagined images.

Eventually the child becomes an adult and, having struggled for many years to find any lasting feeling of fulfilment, may begin to feel within (as you are now) and finds this is constant. The pull to experience is still very strong, so it is unable to hold it for long at first. But at least now it knows where to find the peace it has searched for its whole life.

Soon it is finding it is easier to stay conscious and in touch with feeling complete and has a sense that in some way this space it is feeling is everything. Eventually there is a shift internally as another piece of identification with the body falls away, and the adult is aware, 'My God, I am this! I, this space I have felt my entire life, is the source of all things and I am all there is!'

So the dream continues. The adult has returned to being a child in its state of oneness, but retains all the years of experience of living amongst the forms. Therefore the Enlightened baby has become 'Lord' of its own dream, able to live and enjoy each moment, knowing each may be the last and yet in the knowledge there is nothing to lose and nowhere to go. You are just here to enjoy.

NB. It may be no accident that the words 'Adult' and 'Adulterated' have so much in common, as the purity of the original is lost over time.

Marriage

I am going to get into another controversial area now. Marriage is not as much of a big deal as it used to be, or perhaps it would be more accurate to say 'Not being married is not as much of a big deal as it used to be'. I am going to look at Marriage here. What is it?

Marriage, as we know, is when two people vow in church, before God and before many of their family and friends, often costing large sums of money to themselves and related persons, that they will love each other and remain faithful to the day they die. Doesn't that sound romantic?!

So, what really happens? It is often more than likely they have been arguing about the wedding arrangements right up to the big day, fraught with worry and stress about something going wrong. The day is as stressful as any day could be and, should they get through the day without arguing and falling out totally, they will make their way home or go away on their 'Honeymoon'. They return later to 'normality' where they go back to work to repay the mounting debts from the wedding and get down to everyday living. One does that job or chore, while the other does this. Life quickly becomes about two people living together, sharing the bills, the TV and possibly the sofa (but often not, since it is not uncommon for a married couple to sit in different parts of the house watching different things on different televisions!). If children have not come along already, that is the next step and something else to distract them from the fact that they stopped truly loving each other a long time ago.

Is this a little harsh? I have not mentioned all the situations where the man abuses the woman, or leaves her to go down the pub or the football, gambles or drinks their money away, or has affairs with other women; or where the woman is also having little romances, real or imagined, to make up for what is lacking in their relationship. What has gone wrong?

As usual, it is very simple. We have already seen that love is consciousness, and we also know everybody, almost without exception, is unconscious for most of their waking day. It is hardly surprising the love life is always in such a mess. We can't help but take everything that hangs around our view for more than a few minutes for granted, and THIS HAS TO STOP!! Everything you love can be taken from you at any moment, and you will be sobbing and wailing about what an awful shock it is and how you never expected it and don't know how you will go on etc...

So, why don't you make the conscious decision now to begin to acknowledge and appreciate everything you have in your life, not least of all your husband or wife, and equally how you are not going to put up with them taking you for granted any longer! This has been nobody's fault as such. You just didn't know any better. You got on with living together and the 'living' part became more important than the 'together' part. Do you want some more examples...? Do you still say 'thank you' to your partner for everything he or she does for you? For the cup of tea, the dinner, for carrying the bag, for opening the door, for ironing your shirts, for smiling, for being there, for each and every little thing? If not, why not? Would you not do it, if you were to begin a new relationship tomorrow? If you treated this new person the way you treat your present partner, do you think they would stay, or would they think you were ignorant and ungrateful? And again equally, if this new person was to treat you how your present partner treats you, would you really stay until the day after tomorrow, or have you had enough of this and expect more from a new relationship? Have a look at this for a moment. It is said how wonderful the 'Honeymoon period' is (which may in reality be over long before you actually get to the honeymoon these days), but then we stop making the effort.

Think back, if you are able, to the things you and your husband, wife, or partner used to do with and for each other, but have long since stopped doing. Had you even noticed some of them had stopped? Perhaps you have seen couples together, either in real life or just on television, and had a feeling inside of how lovely it was, or would be, to be that passionately in love (again)? Perhaps so much past has gone now for yourself and your partner that it is too late, or at least that is how it feels.

So, back to marriage... To me, marriage is the idea of true love which comes from the knowledge within as to how it can be, but has been degraded into the unconscious promises and habitual routine of paying the bills and bringing up children. Get married if you want to, but do not see it as an alternative to actually loving your partner, as this is what seems to happen. The woman is with a man she loves and longs for him to love her as she loves him (let's say). He does not know how to, but by asking her to marry him and to be his wife seems a good start; so they will remain together and grow old for ever and ever...

Like this whole book, the answer is to be as aware as you can be of where you are and of what you are feeling. This will keep you present and here and now, and you will be able to see and appreciate the person you are with each moment; just as you will also know they could die or leave you in the next. Is this a negative way to think? Not at all! It is simply appreciating what you have while you have it. It will perhaps amazingly make your relationship much stronger, as there will be no need for you or your partner to have 'one eye open' for an opportunity to love another to compensate for the lack of love between you.

Let me run that last bit by you again. If you are truly able to love, acknowledge and appreciate the person you are with, there is far less chance of them being seduced, coerced or attracted away from you, as they are already getting what they need from you. Of course, if you insist on taking your partner for granted by not loving them, acknowledging them or appreciating them every day in every way, you should not be surprised if they leave you for someone else. If they do stay, you could find you are living with a very unhappy emotional person who is now staying with you through some fear or an obligation to the vows they made many years ago, to stay with you no matter what, 'For better or for worse'. This can become a living hell for one or both parties, so be aware of where you are and of what you are feeling and acknowledge and appreciate what you have while you have it, or you are likely to lose it, in one way or another.

How to tell if someone is Enlightened?

Well, how can you tell? There are stories of Enlightened people performing miracles, being able to describe life after death, being peaceful, wise and generous. But there are also stories of Enlightened people being liars and cheats, amassing huge fortunes, having apparent fits of anger and even sexually abusing children, not to mention the usual practices one hears about with their own students. So what is going on?

You should be getting the idea by now than an Enlightened person is not special. It is certainly unusual to be Enlightened, but that does not mean they suddenly have good morals. If they had good morals before they were Enlightened then these may remain with them, but if they did not have any beforehand, there is no promise they will acquire them. Therefore, you cannot tell who is Enlightened and who isn't from their actions.

It is a little strange to me, because I say this while at the same time am aware my actions are being judged and my own level of Enlightenment may be determined by those who are not Enlightened, according to how they interpret what I say and do. I therefore might decide not to say something in a certain way, particularly in the written word, as people expect me to behave a certain way. If someone emails me and says something like 'You are not Enlightened because there is nobody here to be Enlightened and because you say you are so you can't be; and you charge money and Enlightened people have no need of money!' (as has happened on occasions) it can be tempting to reply 'Then fuck off and stop emailing me!', but then I really would give them another thing to judge me by. Perhaps that would be the 'honest' and therefore 'correct' response, but I usually either don't reply or do so in a careful way to see if I am able to disillusion them of their ideas.

Were you shocked at my use of the language there? Do you still have ideas as to how an Enlightened person would or would not behave? If so, drop them now, because they are not the truth.

I suggest only an Enlightened person can tell if another is Enlightened. This is because they can relate what the other is saying to their own experience. For example, an un-Enlightened person would have to compare the words of one person who says they are Enlightened with the words of another who says they are Enlightened, make allowances for language differences etc, and determine which one seems the most likely, if indeed either of them are. An Enlightened person at least has a solid point of reference. I am Enlightened. If I hear the words of another which seems pretty close, I just listen. If they say no more, then personally I may not know for sure either way. If they go on to say what they have experienced, and do experience at this moment, I can begin to get an idea as to whether they are genuinely where they say they are or not by comparing what they say with what I am feeling at the time. This is possible because, as we have seen, the point within you, the space where you feel complete, is the one space behind all things and as such the experience will be similar in all who truly experience it. Of course, if an apparently Enlightened person tells me they do not believe that they are the only one here and this is their own dream, I have to go on my own experience of realising the one being within me and say, in my own experience, that this person is not Enlightened. This way is the only way I know at this time to tell, besides the stillness or presence that may be felt that suggests an element of conscious experience, but not necessarily all the way to realising as a constant experience 'I am this'.

However, again I say the truth is your own within. Become that and you no longer need to work out who is and who isn't Enlightened. It will be you.

The 'Big Bang Theory'... What is it?

You have heard it said that in the beginning there was nothing and suddenly the universe burst into life in a 'big bang'. Not the most scientific explanation I have ever heard, but from there Science follows the story right through to present day; but let's go back to the beginning. What is this 'Big Bang' when nothing became something? And what was before it?

You could almost answer this yourself now, as you have read all about this dream and how things work here. We have said the space you are feeling is the source and beginning of all that is, where there is no time and no forms of any sort. So how do the scientists describe this point before the 'Big Bang'? Isn't it something along those lines, where there was nothing and then the universe burst into life?

If you were asleep in your bed dreaming and you were looking for the beginning of the dream you were in, that would be as good an explanation as any, wouldn't it? 'There was nothing, and then there was something'. That's the Scientific World's explanation for this one. So, the point before the big bang, the point where there is no time and there is nothing, is the space you feel inside where you are still and at rest and there is no feeling.

So, what about this 'Big Bang' then? Don't forget science views this universe as being infinite and thus imagine there must have been a pretty big bang to create all this. But as you, the individual, begin to feel inside and realise you are this space, you begin to see this 'big bang' occurs every time when you 'wake up' and the dream here is created again.

There is no need to remember this or try to work it out. It will come. Just keep feeling the space inside, which is the same as the space outside. In truth there is no 'inside or outside'. There is just 'space'. Stay with it; there is nothing to lose.

What if my family & friends don't want to do this?

It can be difficult, but first let's have a look at what 'this' is that I am suggesting you do. I have only said for you to 'be aware of where you are and of what you are feeling', so what's the problem? What is the problem to you whether everybody does it or nobody does it? You will see what the problem is, but I am just asking you to look at it.

The problems come from various sides. One side being that you become more conscious and therefore things you have done for years through habit alone fall away; not because you decide to stop doing them, but it was habit doing them and this has been replaced by consciousness. You could also be said to be questioning, perhaps for the first time, what you are doing and how you do it.

Another problem is, as you become more responsible in your own life, you may expect others to do the same. Here you are beginning to see how your own state of mind determines what happens around you and how not to blame others for how you feel, while at the same time you may have some Neanderthal shouting at you and blaming you for hurting their feelings. Were you to try telling them they don't have to blame you, you'd better get ready for the onslaught from their own emotions justifying how they have a right to feel this bad because of what you (or another) did to them; and in their next breath justifying how good it is to be emotional as it is part of being alive! You may wish to tell them to grow up and be responsible, but I don't think this will work either.

Another problem may be nothing more than your eagerness to help and share what you have experienced here. You practice being aware of where you are and of what you are feeling, and find it so peaceful and you feel so complete and life begins to fall into place for you, so you run off like a Jehovah's Witness to 'spread the word'. I'll let you into a little secret 'THEY CAN'T HEAR YOU!!' (...the chances are).

This is because, although this is so simple and indeed is the answer to the world's problems, the World in each person actually likes its problems. Again, you may try to teach others what is in this book on how to deal with problems and begin to enjoy life consciously, but you are likely to receive no end of reasons and excuses as to why they can't do it. Try if you must, but don't get too demoralised if you don't succeed. This is your life. I was only talking to you anyway.

The last problem I can think of here (but there may be others) is your friends may begin to fall away. You may begin to spend less time with them, for no other reason than you don't feel you need to. They may also begin to look to spend less time with you, possibly because they don't find you as 'interesting' as you were. If this happens it is because you are becoming more conscious and thus less emotional. Emotion feeds emotion. If you are conscious you may not be very exciting for the emotions of others. However, on the other hand some people may begin to want to be around you more, simply because you are not as emotional so are more easy-going and nicer to be around (though that's not to say you will want to be around them). Just keep doing it. This is your life. You are not here to live your life through anybody else, or let anybody else live their life through you. Just be aware of where you are and of what you are feeling. Are you doing it now? Aware of your breathing, of the chair, of your legs, body, arms, legs head, face? Do you feel the space and any sensations in the body? That is your truth. That is the only truth. Stay with it. You may feel alone, but you will learn that this is one of the characteristics of being Enlightened. What did you think would happen when you become 'at one' with the universe? You always were alone!

"Be aware of where you are
And of what you are feeling"

Chapter 7

What should you do for a living?

Well, what do you do for a living now? Whatever it is, that is what you should do; until you do something else. There is no 'right' job for a person looking for Enlightenment, or indeed for someone who is Enlightened. For example, at the time of writing this I am still a Rent Officer for a Local Government Authority. Prior to this I was a Debt Collector for a Credit Collection company and my previous positions include a door-to-door salesman and a Nursing Auxiliary for a number of years. So which was the correct job? Clearly all of them were perfect at the time, or I wouldn't have done them.

Quickly I saw my life was here to teach me about me; to enable me to experience what I needed to 'wake up' as fast as I could. This often meant doing jobs I didn't like and even being poorly treated by the employer of the time. But so be it; all was part of the journey into me.

Whatever you do, or indeed don't do, as usual I just ask you to remain as conscious and aware as you can of where you are and what you are feeling, and watch. At any moment it may be correct for you to leave your job, apply for another job, return to work, speak up, say nothing, or whatever else it may be; but you won't know what to do until it happens. It is tempting at times to allow the thinking feeling mind to choose our jobs for us, what to do, when to work, when not to work etc. As much as you can, put this to one side. The whingeing mind wants nothing but to think and whinge and whine about what it wants, but it has no access to the truth behind existence so does not see the full picture. Just stay awake and do what feels right deep inside, and not what you think you want. That is the most you can ever do. That way you are working with life and, as soon as you have learnt what it is you are there to learn, your life will change again. Of course, sometimes we are in a painful situation simply to teach us we don't have to take it, but we have to until we learn this. In the next job we can be learning there are times when we must put up with stuff we don't like. There are no set rules. Just feel within and go with that. You are always in the right place, doing what you are supposed to do.

Would you want to Live Forever?

Strange question..?! I imagine many younger people may reply 'Yes', because this is all still quite new and exciting. Some older people, particularly well past retirement age and perhaps slowing down, may feel that, having seen it all and done it all, the sheer idea of living forever sends shivers through them. I would like us to have a look at the idea though.

So, you are here now, reading this book. I imagine your health is good, but it may not be. You may work and have bills and commitments, or you may be on benefits and still have bills to pay. Every day you see all the problems across the world broadcast on the television and your family and friends battling on, everyone looking forward to the weekend or the holiday, or to this or to that. What if you were to be told now you are never going to die; that you will stay exactly as you are now and live here for ever, and ever and ever and ever? Not for one hundred years, or five hundred years, or two thousand or one hundred thousand, or a hundred thousand, or indeed a billion billion years; you will be here for all time! How do you like that idea? …It scares me!

Well, not a lot, because I know the truth; but the question remains. We fear death, which is natural because the body and emotions always fight to survive, but many would perhaps like the idea of living for ever, without looking at what this would mean in practice.

My suggestion is, the knowledge that we are going to die makes living here bearable. What do you think of that? I say it is the fact that we know we are not here forever enables us to battle on, at least for most of the time, hoping for better times. If you knew, no matter how bad things got, you could spend tens of thousands of years in that situation, I think that would be too much for us and more people would be going mad; withdrawing into their own imaginative world to escape the terrifying reality that there is no escape here. You may think this sounds negative or you may agree, but I just ask you to look at it; that death is perhaps not the enemy we assume it to be. In fact it could be said, admittedly at some times more than others (as it can be tough losing someone we love), death is our greatest companion, as it makes living here possible. I will go into on another page where we go when we die.

Either you Know or you Don't!

What am I talking about here? I am referring to everyone running around debating and arguing about what they think or believe. This is a waste of everybody's time (although it's not really because you have to do something while you are here, so why not debate and discuss the impossible and improvable?). I would like us to look at knowing something or believing it, and what the difference is.

In short, if you believe something to be true, it means you do not know. Can you see this, or has your mind with its arrogance and self-importance got you so convinced and blinded as to its inability to know anything, that you really think, if you believe something is true, it must be? Come on, you are brighter than that! (If this seems harsh, it is because sometimes the mind needs a 'wake up' call).

Let's look at it in simple terms. I parked my car outside the house earlier. I know I did this (as much as it is possible to know anything here), but I only believe it is still there. Likewise, I know I am sitting here now writing this and I believe I will still be here in a little while to finish it, but until it happens I don't know anything.

These examples are related to time and experience, of what I see and feel now and what I don't. Let's say a person tells you they are Enlightened. Are they? You can believe they are, or are not. Neither makes it so. It is just the mind making a judgement according to the information it has now and its own interpretation.

Likewise, you may believe, or indeed disbelieve, what is contained in these pages. The fact is, if you are not Enlightened you do not know, regardless of whether you believe it or not. So, as much as you can, I ask you to reserve judgement of everything here. Both belief and disbelief are still only beliefs, and I am teaching you to realise for yourself your own self-knowledge. Then you will know and will have no need to believe or disbelieve anything, at least with no emotional attachment.

I added the last part because, having told you not to believe anything, this world is built on beliefs. That's ok, but it is important to know the difference and not to get so immersed in the beliefs that you lose touch with what you know and what you don't; as that is the world of arguments, debates and opinions which you are moving away from now. You either know or you don't. You have no need to convince anybody, especially yourself, of anything.

Have you felt you were going Mad whilst reading this?

It could happen. I am talking to the deepest point within you, behind the mind with its beliefs and opinions. This could feel nice, or it could be unsettling; or indeed both. Some people have even gone mad having seen glimpses of the truth contained within these pages (though I will add, not from these pages to date). There is the question again whether I should even write this book at all and, having accepted I will, should I purposely make it obscure and confusing to protect those who aren't ready for the truth contained here? I could indeed have done that, but it seems a shame for me to offer the simplest teaching ever, only to spoil it to protect you from yourself in case you do actually understand it.

So, if you do feel you are slipping away and finding it harder to hold onto some part of yourself, that you are beginning to question, perhaps for the first time ever in any genuine way, what is real and what isn't, don't worry. You are doing well and you are being looked after. Whatever insights or strange experiences that do come, don't fear them, but don't hold onto them either. They will come, and they will pass. Just stay aware of where you are and of what you are feeling. The only thing that can go mad is the mind and emotions. You are the space you feel behind them. Stay with that as much as you can and you will go through it. Feel your breathing again to calm the mind at difficult times, or whenever you remember, and keep going. There is no failure here. (Though admittedly it could be said there is no success either). There is only the dream being lived out according to what is needed. All's well. Stay with it.

Always take Your-self on Holiday

Have you heard this saying? No matter how far you go, you always take your self with you! You are probably beginning to get a pretty good idea of what this means now. Your 'self', in this instance, is your mind and emotions with all your hopes and fears and regrets and wants and resentments. In fact everything you would say that makes you, 'you'. You can go to some paradise island on holiday, or even to live out the rest of your days, but if you still have some or all of the characteristics listed above you are unlikely to get much peace. So what is the answer? Come on, you know by now!

By, as often as you can, 'being aware of where you are and of what you are feeling'; facing problems head on with courage and the knowledge of truth that all is well, holding the space within you, you are actually freeing your-self of all the things above you are holding on to. Whether it is hoping for the future or regretting the past, you will be living now.

Isn't that the dream going on holiday offers us? ...The opportunity to get away and leave all our problems behind? ...Great, though it may take several beers or the like to truly forget, and they are all here when we come back anyway. And besides the individual problems, you are still you, with your own emotional stresses and the likelihood of getting into an argument or upset about something at any moment.

The more you practice feeling aware that you exist, in the knowledge 'I am', the more you are in the place you hope the holiday will provide for you and you are there everyday, more and more. Life becomes simpler and easier as you deal with your problems and you soon don't have any. There are indeed things you have to do, but no problems. You are always peaceful inside and feeling complete and whole. Then you can go on holiday as you wish, but not to 'get away' in the usual sense, but because it appeals to you to have this other experience. Your entire life begins to unfold into a sense of paradise; not always sunny beaches, though that may happen, but more of an adventure playground where you are given every new experience you need as you need it and you let go of each one to accept the next. Just be aware of where you are and of what you are feeling. That is how to 'get away' from your-self, or more accurately to make it more conscious so you don't need to.

So What is the Purpose of Life?

The purpose of living is simply to live out the need to be here, to satisfy the need to exist as a separate entity. Therefore you can see from that, it doesn't actually matter what you do.

You could ask again though, 'Yes, that is my living life, the life I live here, but what is the overall purpose of Life?' ...Sorry. There are no answers!

Does that seem pretty feeble? I can talk of Reincarnation and Karma and many of these other apparently unknown subjects, but get down to the bottom line, 'Ok, so what is the life or space creating this?' and I have no idea. All I have realised is this space 'I' feel inside is the source of all I experience.

I could go on with this page for a while, giving the impression of saying something, but sorry, there are no answers! Just live your life, feel the space and become it; if you do.

"Be aware of where you are
And of what you are feeling"

Chapter 8

What happens when we Dream?

Firstly, there is no 'we'. I am only talking to you (I know you reading this didn't really ask the question, but I do need to get the idea into you that there is no 'we'). Having said that, 'we' still need to communicate here.

We have established there is the space you feel inside, which is the space of intelligence before anything is created. 'Great'. And that space of intelligence we have said is creating all that you see, feel, hear and touch etc. However, this does not always just 'spring' into existence from nothing (though that is the 'big bang theory'). Often the dream begins quite subtly with perhaps abstract images or feelings and then becomes a more structured story line, where the 'dreamer' experiences goings on in a succession of events; not always logical when viewed later. The dreamer sees people, feels scared, happy, worried, may be able to fly, float, or teleport from one place to another, in fact anything is possible at all in a 'traditional' dream. I am of course talking about the dream when you are asleep at night in your bed. Because it is quite close to the space of intelligence you are feeling within which is creating the dream, there is not quite so much identification with the images so it seems even less possible to step back and question what is going on.

The dream then changes to a more solid dream, even further away from the original space of intelligence and into the story it left behind last time. This is when you 'wake up' here. There is a past and a future and established rules and laws of Science, where certain things are possible and others aren't. Here the dreamer is so far away from the source of itself that it identifies totally with the images and experiences it has in this dream. This is where you are now (unless you are already Enlightened). Wake up or stay asleep? Neither really matters. If you do wake up you will only go back to sleep some time, when the dream begins again, so don't worry too much about how you should be Enlightened or should do this or that. Just live your life, whether you are aware it is a dream or not, and be aware of the space within which is your own being. Stay with it. All's well.

What are Psychic Experiences?

You have seen psychics on television telling people things they couldn't possibly know, and you may have even had some experiences of this nature yourself. How is this possible? How can someone know about stuff which happened to someone else years ago, possibly even before the psychic himself or herself was alive? When it is explained it is obvious really (putting aside the fraudsters who are just very clever at reading and leading people).

We have seen there is one intelligence, one consciousness here. That's it! Do you see it? That is the explanation!

Ok, I'll go into it further. There is one intelligence here and you are feeling it inside you. From there everything you experience comes into existence; so why shouldn't one part of the dream have knowledge of another part? On one level you are creating the psychic, the person they are talking to, the audience present and even the television you are watching it on, as it is all in the one dream. On the other level, from the psychic's own perspective, everything is within his/her own mind or psyche so why shouldn't they be able to access whatever they are able to. No big deal really. The information is not always totally accurate or complete, but that's all part of the game here. Nothing is for certain, except the space within where there is no feeling.

While we are looking at this I will mention the other areas of 'The New Age', be it Astrology, Palm Reading, Face Reading, Tarot Cards, Rune Stones, Crystal Balls, Aura reading, Reiki, Phrenology (Head Reading) to name a few. How can any of these be true?

Well, as above, it is very simple. This is one consciousness, one dream, so all is connected. Why shouldn't a person be able (if they have the gift and/or the information) to read the signs in the environment about how things are and may be in the future? Don't worry about it too much. Anything is still something. If you are looking for the truth you will not find it in objects or forms (unless it is a book like this showing you where it is). The truth is the point before anything exists, where you are aware of where you are and of what you are feeling. Enjoy all the other stuff, whatever it is, as you wish. Just be awake (aware of yourself) while you are doing it.

No-Body to Hear

Does a falling tree make any sound when there in no-one around to hear it?

This is an old philosophical question and one which it seems has no answer, because if there is no-one there, then there is no-one to know whether there is any sound or not. It may seem like a silly question, but without meaning to offend anyone (any more than is necessary) many of the philosophical questions are (but most are also able to be answered by an Enlightened person anyway). So, having said that, I do have the answer to this one; and so will you in a couple of minutes. Again, don't try to believe anything here. This is the space within me talking to the space within you. The mind cannot understand this and, even it if it could, it may be unable to cope with it. Just stay with it. All's well.

We have said this is a dream; The Cosmic Dream or The Eternal Dream if you prefer, but a dream none-the-less. If you were in bed dreaming and found a tree had fallen, in your dream, can you tell me if it made any sound when it fell? You may be stuck for an answer, but again it is obvious. Of course it made no sound, not only because there was nobody there to hear it fall, but it never actually fell! You may have been with the tree before it fell, in the sense that you dreamt it standing up and you later dreamt it lying down, but as you never actually dreamt it falling over, it could not have made any noise! You could even dream of a person complaining of having been hit by the tree as it fell, but you know you are only dreaming this person too.

Don't worry too much about this. It is a very deep truth and one you have either realised or you haven't. I was just demonstrating this book is not just 'designed' to answer a specific question and then fall way short if you try to push further. This is the truth whether the individual has realised it or not and therefore will explain anything and everything. Again, just be aware of where you are and of what you are feeling. That is all you have to do.

What about Science?

Where does Science fit into this 'Dream' idea? Ok, let's look at this? ...It fits right here, where it always did. Nothing has changed, just because you may or may not have seen this is a dream. The laws of physics do not automatically crumble just because you know what is real and what isn't. You won't suddenly start flying, despite the old stories of Enlightened Masters levitating. You won't suddenly be able to see through walls or teleport to the moon, or change shape or see into the future or time-travel, or anything else you couldn't do before, unless you do. Again, I add the last part to allow for the knowledge that, although none of the above may happen, you will also know potentially anything is possible.

So, if you are a Scientist, feel free to continue with what you do. If you are a Doctor of medicine or a Psychologist or Psychotherapist or anything else, just carry on doing what you do, as long as you do it. Even when you know this is a dream you still have to do something here, so what is wrong with studying the effects within the dream? After all, I am writing this book and teaching, am I not? ...even though I know 'I' only exist with this dream, writing on a p.c. which is also dreamt so some future person (you), who does not exist where I am now, can read it in some imagined future. So, as I said earlier, "A Dream it may be, But the Dream goes on". Live the dream. Just be aware of where you are and of what you are feeling. You will become more and more aware that only the space is real here. Stay with it. You have nothing to lose.

Promiscuity

Time to get serious again... This subject is one which is an issue in today's society of fast sex and equality for women, sometimes even encouraging them to go 'on the prowl' to be like their male counterparts. But why are people promiscuous? I am going to make some sweeping generalisations here which you may or may not agree with. But again I ask you to reserve judgement and just look at the situation.

I am going to suggest men are promiscuous because they don't know how to love, and women are promiscuous because they are looking for the love which no man has been able to give them. That's pretty general, yes?! But is it true?

Ok, I'll ask the men reading this first, 'Why do you want to sleep around, whether you get the opportunity or not, when each woman you are with has the same anatomy as the next? And even worse still, why is it you can be having sex with one woman while imagining being with another; who may even be no 'better looking' (to you) than the one you are really with!?'

And to the women now, 'What is it you are looking for when you are 'sleeping around'? Could it be for someone to love you, at last, or have you really become so predatory like the men who have slept with you to date, that you are just looking for a quick fix?' (note the word 'fix').

Right, to the explanation... Man's greatest wish is to become whole again inside the body of another, to merge with them physically and psychically. But here, as we know, this has often been degraded to basically satisfying the sexual emotional selfishness by using the body of another, not loving them. For homosexuals the drive is the same except for the attempt to satisfy this need with a body of the same sex. This piece will talk mostly about heterosexuality. If you are male heterosexual your greatest wish is to be inside Woman. However, because the mind is so emotional and always looking for experience, once it has taken for itself what it wants, it looks for the next thing to want. Being present and aware at any moment is hard work and not very exciting. So the man will lust after a woman and once inside her, will go straight for his orgasm and afterwards (or even at the same time) will be thinking about someone or something else. This is particularly likely if he has been with this woman for a while and she is no longer new or exciting to him, and she knows it. However, even if she is exciting to him, she knows he is just going for his own orgasm anyway to please himself, so what's in it for her? And even if she does find a guy who manages not to get too excited so can last longer, it is usually through his thinking about mundane things like his holiday or football scores to keep the feelings at bay, which is still clearly not loving her or giving her his full attention anyway.

Amongst all this stuff the woman doesn't really stand much of a chance to feel loved. Man is so irresponsible, selfish and looking for his own sexual gratification that the woman has two options: Either join Man in the quest for selfish excitement and give up her original idea of being loved as just a fantasy, or resign to having sex when she has to or when she feels a need to be close to someone. When she is able to enjoy it, she is likely to be imagining another man (either real or fantasy) loving her rather than the real one huffing and puffing on top of her, pleasing himself inside her.

Is this too graphic, too straight or blunt for you? How else are you finally going to learn to love and be loved, if you only listen to these Commercial Sex Gurus and magazines who tell you that having 14 orgasms an hour with 18 partners and using 12 sex toys in 15 positions is the way to be really satisfied? What a mess!!!

To the answer, if you are still with me... Be aware of where you are and what you are feeling! (now there's a surprise!). If the man is aware of what he is feeling, in the moment now, he will be able to see, appreciate and acknowledge the lady he is with, without lusting after his own sexual gratification. He can hold her and really love her. She will know she is being loved consciously so will be less inclined to drift off and imagine someone else, or look for her own personal gratification without him. So now both are aware they are together... That's a start at least! Then the man can still be aware of where he is and what he is feeling, but his attention is on the lady, not on himself and thus she feels the conscious energy from him passing through to her. To the extent both are able to stay awake and aware, the stronger the energies, sensations and feelings become, but not through emotional excitement but through true lovemaking. If you are able to do this, you will find, more and more often, both your energies rise together to a climax. But now the climax does not come down. It is an intense completeness and stillness of the two of you becoming one. This is indeed making love in the true sense of the word.

Of course, if you don't believe me or don't want this love, feel free to continue playing with yourself, and others, as you wish; but don't try to convince yourself, or them, that you are loving anybody, whether you are monogamous, promiscuous, or even polygamous. Love is conscious acknowledgement and appreciation and most of all, being aware of where you are and of what you are feeling; and this communicates to the other. If you are a man, perhaps it is time you stopped pleasing yourself. If you are a woman, perhaps it is time you stopped giving in to this pathetic and aggressive excuse for making-love and begin to find the knowledge within you of what it is to truly be loved; because that is the truth. Just because every man you have ever met has been unable to give you the love you want does not mean you are wrong. It just means you thought you had to accept what was on offer. Well no more!! Every time a man has sex with you he takes you a little further away from your internal knowledge of what love is and leaves you a little more empty and wanting. This can lead a woman to despair or to indulging in the predatory nature of the sort that is driving the man to be sex obsessed. The latter then becomes her solitude and it makes a good cover up, for a while.

I shall repeat again what I said at the beginning of this piece "I am going to suggest men are promiscuous because they don't know how to love, and women are promiscuous because they are looking for the love which no man is able to give them". If both you and your partner together want to love properly, he is likely to stop looking around as much at other women because he will be seeing his partner as new every time and really enjoy and appreciate her curves and softness (even though he has seen them a thousand times before); and she will have less and less need to even think about or look at another man, as she is receiving the love she has dreamt about from him and is no longer feeling unloved and unappreciated. There you have Adam and Eve in The Garden of Eden. So, Adam or Eve, can you love enough to be the truth of love that you are, and bring love to life here?

Making-Love in the 'Dream'

So how does Making-Love fit into this 'Dream' idea? The space you feel inside is complete and whole as you know, as there is nothing to speak of and yet everything comes from there. But here it is different. Here is a world of opposites and you are very separate, even if you are Enlightened and feel complete inside. This is demonstrable by the simple fact that the Enlightened person is still here and has a body so has to eat, sleep and go to the toilet etc. So, while you may be aware you are complete in the space inside, here in the dream you are still separate. A body of the opposite sex offers a place where the individual can become one with something within the dream that is representing and reflecting their other half outside the dream. The female energies in its purest form are the stillness of the space within, which is the love every man craves when expressed here in form. The male energies represent the separation within the dream, thus he always has a need to do something; even if it is simply to join bodies with her so he can feel complete whilst still in the dream of being separate. Once inside her they are both complete, as long as they remain conscious and neither drifts off into their own selfish imagination and takes the energies away from the other. When making-love rightly they are united psychically as well as physically.

To the extent you are able to remain conscious and aware in the moment through the building pressure to become lost in the almost overwhelming strength of feeling, you will be able to remain conscious at other times when not making-love. (And again, this does not mean avoiding the situation by dishonestly thinking about something mundane to keep down the feelings. This is not making love either). Likewise, to the extent you allow yourself to become absorbed and lost in the feelings, taking only for yourself and having lost all consideration or even knowledge of the other in the wave of excitement, you will be unconscious the rest of the day as well. Making-love does indeed make you more conscious, while having sex makes you more ex-cited (sited outside) so further out of your senses and unconscious. It is your choice. This is your dream.

"Be aware of where you are
And of what you are feeling"

Chapter 9

Pain and Suffering

What is it and what does it do? Well, physical pain may be simply the result of an existence of separation here, with opposites, extremes and experience. I can only say you need to do what you can to remove the pain through whatever physical means works for you, be it medication, herbs, hypnotherapy or indeed anything else; and do your best to keep the emotion out of it. That means, be aware of what is around you physically and enjoy what you are able, trying not to get too drawn down into the negativity of the problem. This can be very tough, so I am not saying it is easy at all. Just do what you can. Usually, the more you are able to do this, the easier the situation gets, in some way at least.

With regards to emotional suffering, that is something we can deal with. We have seen how we need to be aware of where we are and of what we are feeling (we are also aware there is no 'we' and this is only for you, but I am just making the point). I have said how to deal with emotional suffering but we have not gone into why it is here in the first place.

Emotional suffering is the result of believing you are separate and thus have things to lose and things to gain. When you are complete inside and are aware you have nothing to lose or gain, you are no longer emotional; or at least not in the same way or to the same extent. So, having accepted you get emotional because you believe you are separate and identify with this, why do other people have emotional suffering? You may not be able to see the question at this point, and don't worry if this is the case. All will be come clear(er).

If this is your own dream as I have said, and you suffer because you believe you are separate, when it is you creating the separation, why, when you turn on the television or read the newspaper, do you see everybody else suffering as well? Is it because they are identifying with being separate too?

There are two answers to this, depending on how deep you want to go:

1) Yes, they are identified with being separate too, and hence become emotional about things just as you do.

2) The second answer is deeper and relates to this being your own dream. You get what you need or want according to your own experience. If you need, want or enjoy watching others suffer, life will give you that. (Bear with me. This is about as deep as it gets and the mind will not be able to grasp or accept and certainly not believe this, so don't try; if you can possibly avoid it).

I have said this existence obeys all the rules of a dream. If you were asleep in your bed and dreamt you were surrounded by people suffering, would you be really? Of course you would, in the dream, but you wouldn't know it's a dream so the answer would be at the time 'Yes, there are people suffering here'. And what if you began to see it was only a dream but you could not wake up so were stuck there, and then found you quite enjoyed it anyway so didn't really mind staying (after all, what's the worst that can happen?). You could either withdraw from the 'material' world as some spiritual people have done, finding a quiet place on a hill side or in a forest somewhere, or you could keep your head down and your knowledge to yourself and carry on a 'normal' life, whilst knowing it's only a dream, or you could begin teaching those in your dream that this is only a dream. Of course, you will know you are only dreaming that you are teaching, but that's part of the game. Another part of the dream is you cannot tell these dream people you are teaching that they are not here, as you are dreaming they are and in this dream they are each able to realise they are the only one here and that they are dreaming you. (Are you able to follow this? Don't worry too much. Read it a few times over several weeks and months. Like those 3D pictures, it will begin to become clear).

The point here is, this may or may not be your own dream (and I tell you it is) but, even if you do realise this, you will also see that you are dreaming that everybody else can realise it too. They can't, but you are dreaming they can. That is the truth behind the saying 'Everybody is created Equal'. No matter how hard you try, you will not convince another that they are just part of your dream. If you want to teach them, it must be in love that you are part of theirs. You are not special, even if you are 'God-Realised' (have realised your own being is God).

So, when we come back to the suffering of others, this follows the same rules as the dream scenario above. The answers are, 'Yes, they suffer emotionally because they too are identified with being separate; and that is because you are dreaming they are!'

Again, don't try too hard to get this. I am not sure how much of this is too direct and too blunt and even terrifying if any of the truth does get through. But I called this book 'Enlightenment, the Simple Path', and I will be as simple as I can be (though I may look to soften it slightly). Just stay as aware as you can of where you are and of what you are feeling; that is your truth. There is nothing to understand or work out.

Going through it

Did the contents of the last pages disturb you? Did you get a pang of loneliness? You may not have done. It may have meant nothing at all or you may get a reaction, from that and other pages, as I am talking to the deepest part of yourself. The emotions are the attachment to the experience of being separate, as we have said. When you begin to see that is not the truth, it is like dying. In fact some Enlightened Masters have stated they are already dead, because they have let go of the attachment to being separate and are now in the experience of being complete and whole as if they were dead, but while still in the dream. That's Enlightenment.

So, you may get a reaction reading this book, or you may not. You may get a reaction the first time but not the second, or you might. This is energetic and you are likely to see different aspects and truths each time you read it. If any fear does arise, don't worry. It will pass. Just do as we always do now, and stay aware of where you are and of what you are feeling. That will dissolve the flailing emotion and the feelings will pass after a few minutes. Just stay with it. It is only the emotion seeing it is not really separate, and this means it can't keep up the illusion and pretence much longer. You have nothing to lose really. You are just seeing what is already here.

It's interesting, you would perhaps have thought realising you are 'at one' with everything would make you feel warm and connected, and in a way this is so. But the truth is you actually realise the feeling you are inside is all there is, so being 'at one' does not mean joining with everything else, it means seeing there isn't anything else to join with; or indeed be separate from for that matter!

Are you beginning to wonder again if you really want to be Enlightened? You should. I have not written this book to Enlighten anybody. I write it to expose the truth behind all the confusion so anybody can know what it is and we won't have all this debate and argument about what it is and how wonderful it is to be Enlightened. It is just seeing what is already here, and spoiling the illusion.

Does that sound as though I regret becoming Enlightened? I don't at all, but then I didn't do it to find any answers (which is just as well, as there aren't any). I did it because I had had enough of all the emotional ups and downs and wanted to know if there was a reason behind it all. I was looking for an end to emotional suffering and I found it. But (as you may be beginning to experience) it does mean going through it to find the end, as the emotions fight to maintain the illusion of being separate and their identification with who 'I' am and what I like and what I don't etc.

As you descend deeper into the space within, or put another way, as you dissolve more of the need to be separate, you will go through various uncomfortable feelings, as well as joyous feelings of oneness. Let each pass as neither the positive or negative feelings are the truth. The truth is the space inside where there is no feeling. In fact, that is what Enlightenment is. Just realising 'I' am a space and nothing really exists. Tell me again how much you want to realise you are alone dreaming all this and that there is no-body here really.

NB. For those interested in Buddhism, you may recall the Buddha's own path and driving force was to end suffering. One of his famous quotes on this matter is "Within this fathom-long body is found all the teachings, is found suffering, the cause of suffering, and the end of suffering."

The Human Race

Now back to a light-hearted topic... What actually is the 'Human Race'? Where's the race going?

Of course there's nowhere to race to, as you know. So it's just the movement of going headlong into the world of experience, whether that is achieving or failing, it doesn't matter as both satisfy the need for experience. However, until the need for experience begins to slow, as it may be doing in you as you are reading this book, the quest for greater and greater experience is ever pushing harder for bigger, better, faster, smaller, smoother, coarser, flatter, rounder, noisier, quieter, wetter, dryer, in fact anything other than what is here now.

It has been suggested our race is to explore space... yippee! Yes, you have at the moment the clouds and trees and grass and water and rain and snow and all the animals and amazing wonders to see right here but, as that's not enough, I am sure you want to spend 15 or so years in a metal box travelling through nothing but blackness, trying to find a planet like the one you have left so you can land on it. Or even better, you can help make a glass dome on a barren planet so you can live in that. And you don't think you would want to stick up pictures of the world you left behind with all the beauty and colour(?)

Perhaps the 'Human Race' is the race to populate the world? Well, I think we've done that; don't you? ...But no, many still harp on about the ozone gases and fossil fuels and traffic pollution and disposing of all the waste and generating more and more power and how the natural balance of the world is being destroyed by cutting down miles of rain forests every day. I have yet to hear someone actually say, 'Hey, perhaps if there weren't so many people here, there wouldn't be so much pollution or traffic or waste or need for so much power or to cut down so much rain forest, or indeed any of the other problems?' Oh No... we will keep on multiplying, and keep on destroying this beautiful planet, while looking for another to build our domes on so the 'lucky few' can go and live there instead. (I did say this was going to be light-hearted, didn't I?)

Do you want to be Rich & Famous?

That's the usual dream, isn't it? To be adored by everybody and have all the money in the world, or at least more than you can spend. How does this fit into the experience of Enlightenment?

In short, it doesn't; in the sense that nothing actually changes. One's perception changes so you are not so attached to riches or being famous, but that's not to say you will certainly renounce all possessions and become a recluse, or that you will necessarily drive to take over the world and amass a huge fortune. Either extreme can be the case for an Enlightened person, despite the idea that they would give all their money away if they were really Enlightened. In fact there are many examples of Spiritual Teachers insisting people give them all their money in some form of penance or display of non-attachment to it. This is quite clever, yes? You go to a teacher to be taught, really believing in his greater wisdom and are prepared to follow his instructions, and he tells you to give him all your money to show you are serious. What a farce! Of course he doesn't really want the money (note the sarcasm?); after all, he's a spiritual teacher! (They won't all necessarily claim to be Enlightened) 'What use would he have for money?!!!' (Don't you believe it!).

However, what can happen is this... An Enlightened person is aware this is their own dream, and as such nothing is real. So they may indeed decide there is no real value in material possessions and give them up, to live an apparently barren existence by anybody else's standards. They could also choose to enjoy what the material world has to offer, be it nice cars, a posh house (or four), expensive clothes and in fact anything an un-Enlightened person would enjoy; but all the time knowing none of it is real.

With regards to chasing fame, again an Enlightened person may withdraw and feel no wish to speak to another person ever again. After all, there is no-one else here as every person is only a part of their own dream, so what would be the point of talking to anybody? By way of contrast, another Enlightened person may enjoy the adoration and still seek the fame, while also knowing it is only from illusionary persons within their own dream, but is real enough to enjoy none-the-less. And, as mentioned before, another may seem to live a normal life, appearing to interact on the same level as anybody else.

So, seek fame and fortune as you wish, but again I must say, be as aware as you can of where you are and of what you are feeling. Doing this will keep much of the emotionality out of the wanting and prevent it from spoiling things. This will leave the conscious awareness of what needs to be done now to bring about what you would like, while limiting the amount of disappointment when things don't go as you had hoped and bringing a solution quicker.

As you can see there is no 'right' way for an Enlightened person to live (which also makes it very difficult to tell who is Enlightened and who isn't). Just live your life and do whatever you need to do (though in truth you can do nothing else). The more aware you are, the quicker you learn each lesson and the easier life becomes. It is all about you, not about what you do or how much money you attain, or even anybody else. This is your life, your dream. Enjoy it!

Making your point

How important is it to you that you make your point? Well, however important it is, let it go! Who do you think you are talking to anyway and what does it matter if another person doesn't agree with you or even understand you? (We are talking about the debates and arguments people have and not the doing of a practical task). You'll have to learn to live with it one day, if you are truly going to realise who and what you are, as no-one would believe you if you tried to tell them anyway. Here are a couple of reasons why it is best not to be attached to making your point or winning an argument:

The first is this is your dream, your existence, and as such life gives you whatever you need to experience. While you enjoy feeling emotional, struggling and getting that sense of achievement, that is what you will get. Life will provide for you people (and situations) to fight and argue against, to give you what you want. As you stop wanting somebody (or indeed something) to battle against, life stops giving them to you. It is your choice.

The second is again that this is your dream, so you are actually arguing against a character in your own dream that you are right about something and they are wrong. Now I don't expect you to have realised this already, or even in the next few weeks, but just be aware that you never really win an argument in the way you think. The whole experience is there to give you the struggle, and winning or losing are just the two opposing sides of the same coin that you win every time, whatever the apparent outcome! (You always get the experience).

Just remain aware of where you are and of what you are feeling. This is your truth, the ONLY truth. If you stay in this place where you feel complete already, you will find you don't need to convince anybody of anything. Let people be wrong if they want to be. Who are you to decide they have no right to be wrong anyway? We are all on the journey into our own being. There is no failure here (or even success for that matter).

The World of Television

Television is a truly amazing device. It allows you to escape from the reality of the here and now, without you having to think and imagine any other reality yourself, by absorbing your attention and transporting it into the projected world on the television screen in front of you. The whole family can be sitting in the room watching a film, barely aware for long periods of time of the existence of the room or any of the others in it. I would like to suggest that you practice being aware of the room you are in while watching television. It will be very hard, but the more you practice the stronger you will become and the more conscious you will become at other times.

There is another more sinister reason for me writing this page. The fact that the television makes real for you whatever you need (or want) to experience, without you having to live it physically (in the sense of actually going there or living it). It will project you into the situation and you can share in the experiences of those on the television. That seems harmless, until you have a closer look at what we put on our televisions in the corner of our living rooms. Putting aside the soap-operas which are full of angry, sexual, devious, unhappy, murdering, lying, cheating, resentful, often seemingly 'too thick to be true' individuals, and putting aside the high stress and emotional dramas with their stories of woe and pain and suffering, we then have the news!

So, what's wrong with the news? Nothing's wrong with it, but I just ask you to take a metaphorical step back and look at why you watch the news? We know we are not shown everything that goes on around the world. There isn't time to do that. We know therefore they select which stories to show and which not to. Sounds fair? Now, whether you believe in conspiracies and cover-ups and media-brain-washing or not, we are agreed on the fact that we will not hear about the entire goings on around the world, no matter how long we watch it for. There is also the fact that, as the whole world is so emotional and unhappy, the news that makes it to the papers and television are all stories of more pain and suffering, the more shocking the better, to add to your own. Sounds great, doesn't it? Great for the emotions that always want you to be feeling something!

I want you to see that you watch the news for entertainment, at least as much as to find out what is going on around the world. 'We' (people) often sit in our armchair in our comfortable house with a big plate of food and drink in one hand, watching the images of the latest bombings, murders, rapes, brutality, lies, cheats, and numerous horror stories and disasters. We remark on how awful it is, go 'Tut, tut' every now and then and 'Ahh, isn't that awful', and then when it has finished watch the comedy afterwards and forget all about it; until we watch the same images again before we go to bed and say the same comments. We may even send a fiver to satisfy our emotional feeling of guilt and then get into our nice car and drive to the local supermarket to spend a small fortune on groceries.

I am not saying we all do the above, but I am just asking us to look at the hypocrisy of watching the television so we can see others suffering and trying to convince ourselves we are doing them a service in doing so. We know they are suffering. This is a world of suffering. If you are moved to go out to one of these countries, or indeed a local area, which needs help, great! But for most of us there is no movement at all to help in any way at all, except for the arrogance to think, while I am stuffing my face with my pork chop and swigging a beer, that my sympathies for these poor people are actually doing them some good.

So watch the television, and watch the news if you do. But just be aware that you do have a choice. Also be aware that feeling and dwelling in the emotions within you only feeds the emotions more. That is to say, while you enjoy watching the pain of others and feel the sympathy (after all, what else are you going to do for them?), you will have more trouble controlling your own negativity at other times. You will get back what you put in. Fill your head with negativity and you find that is what you are carrying around with you. The more you can feel the space where you are complete and at peace, the easier your life will be.

Perhaps you are offended by this; by being told you enjoy watching the suffering of others? Ok, so why do you watch it? Are you forced to, or is there something in you that feels compelled to watch? At least admit that you watch it because there is something in you that wants to watch it, even if it is to feel sorry for the people. If that's the case, then you watch it because you enjoy feeling sorry for them, in the same way we watch any drama or movie, be it funny, or scary or sad. The news is just another drama the emotions feed off. Just don't put the fact that you watch it onto the poor sods whose suffering you are watching, and don't allow your mind to delude yourself into believing it is actually doing them any good at all by feeling sorry for them. If you are that sorry, get up and do something about it.

There is of course the other point that as this is your dream (which you may not know yet) and therefore anything you watch on the television is also dreamt, as is the television. Everything here is for your own entertainment, be it for positive or negative feelings, it gives you feelings none-the-less. Enjoy what you do, but stay aware while you do it.

If you are disturbed by the above and are adamant that watching the news assists those portrayed on it, I would like to suggest something else to you. If you really want to help reduce the suffering in the world, you could start by reducing the amount of emotional suffering, with its judgements and justifications for how it feels and who it accuses and blames for what it goes through, within yourself. When you are around other people you may think your emotions don't do any harm, but you are polluting the space and atmosphere with your negativity and we have to live in it. (Well, we don't, as you are creating us as well, but if you accepted that, you wouldn't mind the bit about the news either). So, again I suggest you do your best to be as aware as you can, of where you are and of what you are feeling. This will keep your own space as free of suffering as possible and this peace and easiness will pass on to those around you. Then if you want to watch people starving on TV, read about who was murdered or raped today, who did what or who got away with what; whether you want to go down the local hostel to offer to help, or give up your job and go to Africa or sit in a rubber dinghy in front of a Whaling ship, you can do whatever you like. But please, do it from a position of conscious peace and awareness and not from pain inside looking to make up for a lack of something.

"Be aware of where you are
And of what you are feeling"

Chapter 10

Living in the Now with Children?

Perhaps you have wondered, how the hell do you stay aware and conscious while dealing with children? Well, it's not easy, but it does get easier. In fact everything gets easier, the more you do this. You will find, when your child does something, you will now be more aware and better able to deal with it at the time in a firm but fair way. The usual way is often for parents to ignore it, or respond but not whole heartedly, until the child has been doing the thing for so long that the parent explodes in emotional rage. It is much easier for the child if it knows the rules. If you are consistent and fair and do not appear to lose control, they learn a sense of self-control and fair-play. So by staying aware of where you are and of what you are feeling, you are better equipped to cope with the emotional tantrums of children, as it no longer stirs your own (it gets less over time) and you are now able to teach the child that these tantrums are not acceptable. After all, if they are allowed to behave that way as children, the emotions don't go away as they get bigger; they can just do more damage. I would even go as far as to say, now you know these things, it may be the job as parent to begin to teach the child how not to lose control when it doesn't get what it wants. This is a pretty good lesson to learn in this world, where one's own emotional state determines what happens in one's life!

So, it can be done, whatever you are doing. It is you after all. It does not leave you just because you are busy or having a tough time. It is in such times you most need to work as hard as you can, to hold onto the knowledge that you exist and not lose your-self in the emotion. Having said that, life does give you the experiences you need to learn and often these experiences are pretty tough, involving being aware while the emotion is dying to get out and rant and rave and go into the imagination of the situation. Again, stay aware. We are not talking about suppression of feelings here, as that just buries them. We are talking about just feeling them, taking the action that needs to be taken, and then denying them from going into the imagination to relive and relive and relive the situation over and over again. This will take the emotion out of the situation making it easier to cope with, if it is still there at all. Stay aware. That is your only job, besides living your life.

Coincidence and Deja-Vu

We are always amazed when we witness a coincidence which seems too good to be true, when a combination of circumstances fall into place to bring about a result as if the whole lot was engineered by one intelligence. We also get feelings of recognition that we have experienced a situation before. How does this happen?

I gave the answer away a little with the "... as if the whole lot was engineered by one intelligence...", because now you know it is. You already know there is one intelligence here creating everything that happens around you each and every moment. Perhaps the amazing bit is you don't notice it more often. We are generally so unconscious and lost in our own attachment and self-delusion of being separate, that we can be amazed and even frightened when we see some of the coincidences that occur. For that split second we have to face the possibility that this is not as random as we like to believe. But this does not stay with us long, as we quickly lose ourselves again in the familiar goings on which do seem unconnected and re-affirm our belief that it was an amazing fluke, a 'one off' that happens every once in a while.

The more you practice being aware of where you are and of what you are feeling, you will come to know there are no 'coincidences' as it is your own 'mind' creating everything. You will begin to notice more and more 'little' things you would normally not have noticed, as life works with you to give you the experiences you need.

With regards to deja-vu, the same applies. This is your own consciousness dreaming this. Why shouldn't you occasionally get the feeling that something is familiar or you have lived that moment before? You are after all creating it now!

Where do you go when you die?

Have a wild guess... "Nowhere?" ...Yes, well done. There is nowhere to go!

Do you understand this? If this is a dream, when the dream ends, the dream ends. There is nowhere to go. Of course, if you need to continue with this, or indeed another dream, fine, it will continue for you; but it is still a dream.

But that's ok. There is nothing wrong with dreaming (if there was, none of this would be here) and there is nothing wrong with enjoying it. It just makes it less painful if we know it's not as real as we think; but having said that, if we are still in the early stages of our dream 'career', we may not be ready to give up enough of the attachment and wake up enough to see this yet. That's ok too. There is nothing really to lose here. 'You', the space you feel inside, cannot really die. The dream just fades once you have experienced all you need to. Should it still be in you to join up with your loved ones 'on the other side', that is what you will do. Should you need to go to a higher astral plane and float around for a few millennia, then that is what you will do. Whatever you need, you will get. Likewise, if you are filled with anger and fear and really strong attachment to circumstances here, it is possible the psyche could semi-remain here in a dream state, replaying experiences over and over again, and the people in your dream would call you a ghost. Eventually even that need would be satisfied and you will move to another dream (or the dream will change) to something more fulfilling. The point is, you will always get what you need. As a general rule, most are likely to let go of their attachment here as they die and connect more with their being and feel complete and whole in a way never experienced before. In this state you have no need to long for those you have left behind, as you don't feel you have left anything behind as you are complete. Feel the space now... You are already complete!

'You tell me; this is your dream...' Do you get the point? Whether they exist or not, or whether the planet Mercury exists or not, or whether your car is still outside your house or not, is all part of your wonderful dream. You may see an Alien tonight. You may go on their space-ship and be transported within a few seconds to their planet on the other side of the galaxy, have a cup of tea and an alien scone and be back in time for work tomorrow ... anything is possible!

That is not to say you should, or you shouldn't investigate this area, or any other if you are moved to. You can dig holes as an archaeologist to learn about the past, even though you will know it is only a dreamt past, but what's wrong with that? You could divide up the atom to find what is inside it, or send satellites into space and watch the planets through a huge telescope. You can even just do your 9-5 job without a care in the world about the history within this dream and what is 'out there'. Everything is within you anyway. This is your dream. You live and enjoy it as you wish. Anything is possible. (That's not to say it will happen. Some things may even be highly improbable, according to your experience; but that's not to say it's impossible!).

So, do aliens exist? I do not believe I have seen one and I can't see one now; but many say they have. I have a mild interest in the area, but nothing more than that. If I do go off and have an alien-scone on some far off planet, I'll let you know.

Senile Dementia

Have you ever heard the saying, 'Going through your second childhood'? Do you know what it means? We have said the child is living in the moment and 'at one' but is not aware of it; it just is. It then grows up to lose its conscious connection with its being and is absorbed in the world of objects. After sixty or seventy years (let's say) of struggling in the world of separation, it can happen that the person begins to withdraw from their attachment to the world of objects, with the fixed idea of time, to find themselves again living in the moment with little or no idea as to who or even where they are. They are actually returning home, but there is still enough emotion left to get disturbed and worried by this new experience, of being 'nothing'.

It is common for friends, family and even care-staff to try to coax the elderly person back to 'reality', back to their memories of who they are. This often leads to upset, as the person is told about all their family who have died and that they are a confused old person in an old people's home. Perhaps it is sometimes better to allow them to be who they are, even if they don't know. If they ask if they've got school today, tell them it's Sunday. If they ask where someone is, say they've popped down the shops. If they really have lost touch with the 'reality' here, telling them the truth may only cause more confusion. Once they have forgotten what you have said, the emotion of being confused and distressed is likely to remain anyway; but they won't remember why.

So, getting old and senile is not really a bad thing. It is just returning to the innocence of being a baby again, before totally letting go of the dream which has caused so much pain and heartache and loss for so long. If this is you, don't worry. You are nearly home.

Grief

I know I talk about this only being a dream, but we all know, dream or not, it really hurts to lose someone you love. So, where does grieving for a loved one fit into this? Depending on what you have experienced, either prior or during reading this book, you will know the answer already.

Firstly, you need to acknowledge and appreciate the person while you are with them. If you don't, you are likely to feel there are all sorts of things you should have said but didn't, because you thought you had time. If you always acknowledge and appreciate what you have, when you lose it, it will not be such a shock.

Let's say you have lost someone recently. This is awful and you feel the pain of separation, as if you can't go on; in fact you are sure it's not worth going on. Without them to talk to, be with, you feel there is no point anymore. What can you do?

Without meaning to sound blasé about this, you need to be aware of where you are and of what you are feeling. What you have lost is indeed painful and this is real, but the space inside you is also real. You will feel the pain when you do this, but you will also feel the peace behind it as you are aware, behind the pain, you are complete and you still love them. Your love has not gone.

Do you want to keep thinking about them? Stop! Do you want to look at their photographs or things they have made you? Stop! You are feeding the belief that you are separate and in that you are feeding the emotional pain that is revelling in the feeling of being separate. You are complete, in truth. You love the person and in that space inside you, the love is still there. If you allow your emotions to take you away and into your world of imagination, you will feel incomplete and will continue to do so.

To stay aware of where you are and of what you are feeling will be especially difficult in times of loss (of anything), but is also the most powerful time to do it. It will be tempting to listen to the mind that tells you the memories and photographs are all you've got left of them and to stop looking at these would be unacceptable and unforgivable; but it is what you need to do if you wish to regain the feeling of love and being complete. You will not stop loving them. In fact you will find you always love them as the knowledge of them is still within you; but not the pain of being separate from them which is what the memories, thoughts and pictures tell you. Stay with it, even when it is tough (especially when it is tough). It does get easier. You are being looked after. You cannot be abandoned, even if it feels as though you are. This is your life, and all is ok.

"Be aware of where you are
And of what you are feeling"

Chapter 11

Enlightenment in Men and Women

Just a brief note to say the experience of Enlightenment, or more accurately the process leading up to it, is certainly not the same for everybody. Some receive many insights over several years, as happened here. Others seem to have a sudden shift in consciousness and apparently find themselves Enlightened (though often quite a lot of inner searching has happened prior to this point). There is no need for you to have the same experiences as anybody else. This is your life, your dream. You will experience what you do, and only when you need to. Do not allow the mind to judge what experience you should, or should not have. Just be aware of where you are and of what you are feeling; that is your only task.

I thought I'd mention in case the question arises, the experience in Woman may be particularly different from that of Man. This is not because she is any less Enlightened, but because it is more of a 'full being of love and oneness' and less of the intellectual knowledge and information as contained in these pages. That is also why the Masters are all male. I know of very few female 'spiritual teachers' and one I have heard a little about apparently never speaks when holding meetings.

The bottom line is, don't decide what you should be feeling or where you should be 'spiritually'. You are feeling exactly what you should and are exactly where you are supposed to be. Of course this can all change in the next moment so don't decide it should stay like this either. Keep going. There is nothing to lose. Just enjoy being where you are as much as you can.

Excitement Vs Passion

Is there a difference? To me 'ex-cite-ment' is to be unconscious and out of my senses, lost in the whirlwind of feelings which take over and the person loses control. Passion is having the strong feelings, but still being conscious and aware and not becoming lost in them. Therefore you are able to enjoy them with no need for them to continue any longer than they do. There is no wanting for more when the feelings start, during, or after they finish. Just conscious enjoyment of what is, with no opposite.

Excitement itself consists of opposites. It could be exciting in a good, exhilarating way, or exciting in a frightening, shocking, unhappy way. Then it has its own opposite, which is boredom, when there is not enough excitement to keep the mind entertained and it looks for more.

If you are lost in your senses when times are 'exciting' in a seemingly good way, you will find you are not be able to hold onto your senses when things go bad and not your way. As we have said before, everything must be paid for and what goes up must come down. If you allow yourself to get excited, you will pay for it later. You will be knocked from one side of the excitement spectrum to the other as circumstances change, and yearn for something to happen when nothing seems to be happening in the quiet periods as the mind wants more experience.

You may of course enjoy all the passion as you do, while it is felt here, as it has no opposite. By remaining conscious it the moment and simply enjoying 'what is', you do not perpetuate the swinging pendulum of emotions. This is indeed a wonderful dream and you may enjoy what you can. Just be aware of the law 'Everything must be paid for' and enjoying 'excitement' is playing amongst opposites and extremes, and you will always want more..

The Bible

Whether you accept the stories of Jesus in the Bible to be fact or consider them to be just usurped Pagan stories, many contain the truth none-the-less.

There are sayings such as 'Be still and know that I am God' and 'I and my father are one'. There are also stories of people being tested to see how far they will go, to do what they 'know' to be 'right' against all other evidence and experience.

You too will feel like you are being tested at times. You will know something feels right. You will see no evidence to support the feeling, but will know you must do it. This is likely to go against even your own emotional feelings and leave you in an apparent turmoil. On the one side there is what your inner knowledge is telling you, and on the other side you have what your emotions, and indeed possibly everybody else is telling you. I will bring you back to the quotes above. Your highest truth is the space inside. This is where everything begins and ends. Feel it as often and as much as you can, being aware of where you are and of what you are feeling. The truth is indeed within you.

God works in Mysterious Ways

Does He really? Or are you starting to understand God's ways now? Perhaps you think it is blasphemous of me to even suggest this? If you think the latter, then you have not got the point of this book; which was to show you the space you feel inside, where you feel complete and whole, IS GOD. That is why Enlightenment is also called God-Realisation. It is to realise God within you.

So, back to the 'mysterious ways' bit. We like to think we should have what we want, and as we live in our own personal minds and selfish emotions we really struggle to understand what is going on here. As you begin to experience more the space inside as being the same space of intelligence creating everything, the ways aren't so mysterious anymore. As I have said many times in these pages, you always get what you need, but not what the selfish mind with its attachment to being separate, wants. You need the experience of being separate, so you have things given to you to make you feel complete for a moment and then they are taken away so you can feel separate. You like to feel anything as long as it is something, so life gives you no end of things to think about, worry about, and hear and watch and read about, to make you feel something. As you want less to feel so separate, you find less things happen to make you feel so separate. And the less you identify with the feelings when these things do happen, the less and less they occur; until your whole life is a flowing of your own conscious need to exist, but without the pain of being separate. See? Not so mysterious really? ...is it?

God and The Devil

Two names we hear when discussing Religion. You know who or where God is by now, but what about The Devil?

In the Bible 'The Devil', Lucifer, was God's right hand Angel and was cast down to Earth as he thought he could do a better job than God. Does this sound familiar? Isn't that what your mind does all the time...? Think about how things should be other than how they are? That is why I tell you to 'be aware of where you are and of what you are feeling'. This prevents you from going into the imagination and judging and thinking how things are wrong, so you can feel the space where all is right. That is to say, you are feeling the moment and are therefore in line with 'God's will'. The truth behind the story of 'The Devil' as you can see, is your own thinking selfish mind that is never satisfied and always looks to please itself through any means it can think of. The only way it can ever be satisfied is when it gets tired of fighting all the time. Then it relaxes the pressure a little for you to feel the space behind, 'God', which is your own complete being and it was here all the time. Just be aware of where you are and of what you are feeling, as often as you can, and keep doing it. That is all you need to do!

Possession and Channelling

A bit of a change of subject here, to the increasingly popular subject of Mediumship. What is it? And do they really channel other spirits?

Firstly, who are these other spirits? You know now that this is your own dream, so all the people around you are dreamt too. Ok; so when you dream here that you meet a person with this 'ability', it is not impossible for them to connect with another dreamt personality, within the one being, and allow that to operate through their (dreamt by you) body. It is also not surprising at all if the Medium can tell you things only that dead person would know; is it? It is all the one dream within the one mind anyway.

If you have this ability to channel, be careful. In order to do this you must go into a trance like state (at least in the beginning) to step aside and allow the other personality to enter and take over your body. This book is about connecting with the truth behind your own personality. To make way intentionally for another personality to take your body over is pretty far removed from what we are doing here. The more you can feel the space inside where you are complete, you will realise this is the truth these other entities were not able to connect with, while they were in a body. That is why they are still floating about trying to take over yours. They want another chance to experience being separate in a body in a way that being in 'spirit' does not give (as they are closer to the truth so are not so separate). So, give your body to other dreamt personalities as you wish, but the truth of all life here is the being you feel where there is no feeling, when you are conscious and awake.

While on this subject, I have just been reminded of 'Ascended Masters'. Can you see what these are? They are clearly not Masters at all, are they? Let's say you become Enlightened and become The Master, which just means you have become the one consciousness behind the dream. When you die, the dream ends as you know. Do you really think you will feel a need to create such a faint far off version of this again, to give these other dreamt (by you) personalities information about the truth? ...Because that is what is being claimed. No, once the Master has died, you do not 'hang around' waiting to be channelled; as there is nowhere to hang and no-one to channel you. You simply woke up from your dream. (I am aware you probably were not be able to answer the above rhetorical question, but you will one day).

So, just be as aware as you can, of where you are and of what you are feeling. That way nothing can take you over, be it another 'spirit' entity, or just a plain old mood or bad feeling. Stay aware. Be the Master.

"Be aware of where you are
And of what you are feeling"

Chapter 12

That is the order of events when going deeper into inner truth. First you might intellectually understand some of the ideas here, but that is not true knowledge at all. Anyone with some amount of mental capacity can understand what I have written here. The change happens as you begin to feel something different. When there is a deeper sense or a flash of information, which then leaves you. For certain parts of the self-knowledge it is likely you may receive the same insight a number of times, each reaffirming the last. Eventually it will remain available and you will have access to it at any time you are reminded, but for most of the time you will forget it totally and live as you did before. Nothing has really changed. You just have a little more knowledge as to what is real and what isn't.

Experiences will come and go as you sink deeper into your own truth, the space you feel now where you are aware you exist. One day, should it be right, all the experiences, knowledge and insights may come together in one experience, described best as 'I am this'. The space you have felt your entire life, the same space you have been practising feeling ever since fist picking up this book, merges with the space outside you to become one space. In fact there is no longer any 'inside' or 'outside' of you. There is only 'This'. The space you are feeling is it! There is nothing else to do, no-where else to go, no-one to follow, nothing and no-one to believe in or convince of anything. The space you are feeling is all that is here. There are still images, but that is all they are now, just two dimensional images within your own mind.

As with every other experience, this too will pass; but eventually it becomes a constant experience of being 'this'. However, because it is simply the process of becoming the space behind the forms, there is nothing to feel here, so there is no experience. There are no flashing lights or floating or appearing or disappearing. Not even any real answers. There is only the becoming of the space you have been your whole life, and nothing more. So you can see, hopefully, while it is good to have the information that the answers exist, should you want them, I suggest it does not matter at all if you don't have them yourself at this time. There is no glory in being Enlightened! No great Godly outlook or blissful experience of union and oneness at all times, as there is no longer anything left to be 'in union' with and nothing to be 'at one' with. There is also no longer anything to be separate from, so there is really no experience in it at all most of the time. It is just being aware you are dreaming this and in that you are alone, getting on with whatever you want to do while you are here until the dream ends and you disappear. So don't search for Enlightenment. There is nothing here! Just be aware of where you are and of what you are feeling. This will help you deal with the apparent separation without the pain, helping you feel complete while you live the dream. And live the dream you must, it is after all your dream. What else are you going to do? (If you answered 'commit suicide' to that question, the emotion will only create another dream. There is no escape, but you have nothing to lose; and nothing to gain).

Is that frightening to you? Does that give you a sense of what is going on here? (This may be too blunt and too straight, but that is the nature of this book. I am not going to confuse you to protect you, but I will try to explain it to you, to show you it is ok.) You are stuck, apparently, in this world of pain and separation and looking for a way out. However, you have found it, and it is not what you had thought or hoped for. So, your choice is, either focus on this emotional world of pain and separation where you have lived for so long, or on the world of peace where 'I' am alone'. Pretty lousy choice, yeah? Well, it could be, but as you become more aware of the space, you become less attached to the shapes and the idea of being separate anyway. It is the pain of being separate that is also afraid of being alone. As you become free of one, you lose the fear of the other.

If it is of any interest to you, my own fear, once I had seen and accepted I am alone here, was the opposite. I was trying so hard to wake up and leave the nightmare of a dream behind, that when I was told it could start again once the being ('I') am fully awake, this thought terrified me. I thought, 'How can I be so stupid, to forget how painful it is here that I would really start another dream? That was a number of years ago now and the fear has gone. I now love being here in my own Garden of Eden. I am with a woman who I am loving rightly and she is realising her own truth through our love. Life gives me what I need to experience and I learn lessons fast; so they move on fast. Every moment is perfect and it is a pleasure to be alive here; even if it is my own dream. So, whether I stay in the dream, or the dream evaporates and there is nothing here, all is perfect. It could be nothing else.

Human Nature

By now you should be under no illusion as to what Enlightenment is. So, do you still want to pursue it? It's ok if you do. I did; so how can I tell you not to? You have all the tools and information you need right here, except for being in person with a person able to demonstrate the experience. The truth reflected to you by this book is very strong, clear and direct, but it is not the same as being in front of a person living in this state, able to answer your questions in your own experience.

You know what Enlightenment is now and what it isn't, and even what is required to do it ie... 'Nothing'! Just be aware of where you are and of what you are feeling. That shouldn't be too hard; should it?

In practice, this is the hardest thing in the world to do. This world, this dream, is built on the attachment or love of being separate. As we have said, there is nothing wrong with that. The problem comes when we want to be complete inside while being separate out here. This is quite a neat balancing act and I feel now as if the whole purpose of the dream was to get to this place; where I can still be separate and experience all the wonders here, but be complete inside so do not get hurt by believing the separation. All that work for all those years, all that struggling and effort through the separation of pain and suffering, just to enjoy the last part as I am finally waking up!

So, it is not easy at all. The pull to be lost in the dream of objects and feelings is very strong. It is Human Nature to search and struggle and achieve. To lose and find and conquer and grow and do all the wonderful things people do here. It is not in our 'nature' to feel the space inside and feel nothing. Don't be too hard on yourself, if you do find it difficult. It was always going to be, until it isn't any longer.

That reminds me of the saying that 'Enlightenment is effortless, but it requires effort to get there'. By way of quick explanation for this: it does indeed take effort to hold it for any length of time. But you will find the more you do hold it, the more you will 'catch yourself' being lost in your imagination and bring yourself back to the here and now. You may tell yourself off for this (which is another clever trick of the mind and emotions, to get you to think about thinking and feel bad. Then you feel bad about feeling bad about thinking etc). As time passes you may catch yourself more and more and even start to believe you are thinking more than you did before. Actually you are just catching yourself more often and the time between 'coming back to your senses' is getting shorter. Eventually, whatever it is that is reminding you to 'wake up' is there all the time. You no longer have to try to stay awake, because you haven't gone anywhere. You are indeed 'already awake'. Stay with it and keep going. Life, your own space and truth inside, is looking after you. You are ok.

The Purpose of This Book

So, what is the purpose of this book? It has possibly been a bit of a roller-coaster ride for you, as you have seen and experienced different things. At times you may have felt fear or elation or peace or oneness. Each page has a different tone and vibrates or relates to a different part of your-self. You may have been forced to look at and question different areas you would have preferred to have left as they were. You may have had glimpses of the truth, that this is indeed your own dream, and this has scared the sh*t out of you. That's ok too. This whole book is to tell you, it's ok. It's ok not to be Enlightened. It's ok to have problems and it's ok now if you want to deal with them and work through them. It's ok to wake up and be Enlightened, but it's ok to stay asleep. Whatever you do, is ok, because this is your life.

This book was to show you the truth. To show you there is a real place where you are complete and whole, and it could even be said 'immortal'. It is true you are separate whilst reading this and you may be Enlightened but are probably not (as most people aren't) but you know that is not the truth. The truth is you are already complete and whole and, should you ever want it, this place is always here for you. It couldn't be any closer to you. It is the space you are feeling now.

Read this book as often as you are moved to. Each time you read it you are likely to experience something new as it talks to the deepest part of you. This will bring your own knowledge to the surface, allowing you to realise it for yourself. These pages have been written from the deepest part of my being, which is your being. This book is for you. It is your story, your truth, your dream. Sweet dreams. I will be out here while you need me, and in here (in the space) when you don't.

Three Simple Steps to Enlightenment

1) Be aware of where you are and of what you are feeling
2) Start Now!
3) Keep Doing it!

Have you got it?
Do you need to read it again?

Acknowledgments:

Thank you to the many people who have influenced the development of this book. This includes those who have simply asked questions over the months via email and in person at talks or meetings. Also to all those who gave advice and assistance when we set up the website and to those involved in arranging or permitting my appearance at the various venues. Thank you also to those who were directly involved in the practicalities of creating this book, from suggesting topics to cover, to finding a publisher, to proof-reading the manuscript; and finally to Dr Nitin Trasi and Johannes Tsurkka for their comments to be included in the finished article. The book seemed to almost write itself over only four weeks, with my just sitting in front of the pc evenings and weekends, and this trend continued to publication with events following on, one from another, apparently seamlessly. Thank you to all. This is indeed a book created by all, for the one.

For information on Nick's Talks, Teaching classes, One-to-Ones and other publications,

please visit www.nickroach.co.uk
email: enquiries@nickroach.co.uk

Or write to: Nick Roach Teachings,
PO Box 429,
West Byfleet,
KT14 7XA,
UNITED KINGDOM